I0828535

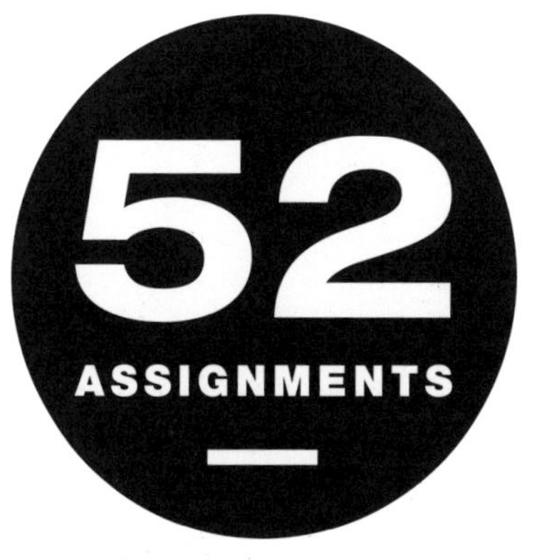

BLACK & WHITE
PHOTOGRAPHY

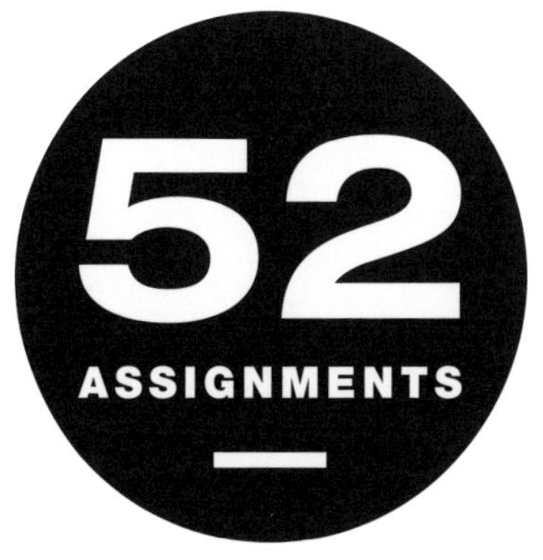

BLACK & WHITE

PHOTOGRAPHY

BRIAN LLOYD DUCKETT

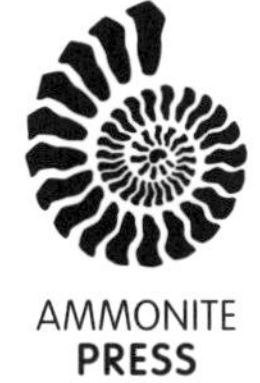

ASSIGNMENTS

Tick off your completed projects

ASSIGNMENT KEY

Each assignment has symbols showing the type of tasks involved.

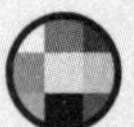 LIGHTING

 CREATIVITY

 STREET

 LANDSCAPE

 TECHNIQUE

 PORTRAIT

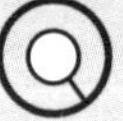 DETAILS

 LOCATION

ASSIGNMENT JOURNAL

Use the journal spaces throughout the book to keep a record of your experimental assignments and images.

INTRODUCTION

For those of us lucky enough to have grown up in the era of black and white, it feels quite natural to see the world in shades of gray. My first taste of "real" photography was at the age of 13, and the visceral experiences of those early days of emulsion, darkrooms, and chunky metal cameras remain with me today. Fast-forward 30 years and, as a documentary and street photographer, black and white still plays a big part in what I do, whether it's shooting on film or using digital gear.

Before we go any further, we should explore a couple of technical concepts. Firstly, what is monochrome? And how is it different from black and white? Monochrome images contain various shades of a single color. When we refer to "black and white," on the other hand, we usually mean "grayscale," or a range of gray tones. However, nowadays, "monochrome" and "black and white" are often used interchangeably (as is the case in this book) to describe an image containing shades ranging from the darkest black to the brightest white.

Secondly, should we shoot in color and convert to black and white in post-processing, or should we convert in-camera? While there's no right or wrong approach, my personal preference is to shoot in Raw, giving me much more flexibility in the treatment of the image later. If I have the option of shooting in both Raw and Jpeg, I'll often set the Jpeg to Monochrome mode, which will help me to visualize the final image.

So, why shoot in black and white at all? Understanding the medium of black and white will take you a long way toward understanding photography, not least your ability to simplify compositions and to evaluate light. These gifts will even help you to become a better color photographer. Just look at the work of some of the great black-and-white photographers: Ansel Adams, Henri Cartier-Bresson, Richard Avedon, Daido Moriyama, Don McCullin, David Bailey, Sally Mann, Irving Penn, Josef Koudelka; there's no shortage of outstanding photographers who saw black and white as a creative choice rather than a technical constraint. And that's precisely how you should see it.

I have structured the 52 assignments in this book to help you become familiar with this wonderful medium, squeezing every last drop out of the potential of using black and white to produce superb images. Whether you're like me—a street photographer primarily interested in the content of an image—or you're more of an Ansel Adams, striving for aesthetic perfection, I hope these assignments will make you fall in love with black and white and all it has to offer.

Brian Lloyd Duckett

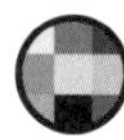

TECHNIQUE

- A focal length of 80–120mm will produce the most flattering effect.
- Try to find the biggest window you can, ideally not facing direct sunlight.
- Think about when to shoot: these portraits work particularly well later in the day when the light is softer, creating more pleasing skin tones.

► *Try to add context to your images. This gentleman was an avid crossword solver, so the newspaper was deliberately chosen as a prop.*

MOMENT IN THE SUN

Natural light can help to produce the most stunning portraits and they can look particularly characterful when shot in black and white.

For this assignment, you'll need a willing model and a good source of soft light, ideally a south-facing window (the bigger, the better). You don't need a professional model—just ask a friend or family member. If your subject isn't used to posing for photographs, they may feel stiff and uneasy. They'll be much more relaxed if you get them doing something they're familiar with, such as writing or holding a book.

Place your subject close to the light source and experiment with the positioning so that you get just the right balance between light and shade on the face.

In terms of exposure, try exposing for the highlights and don't worry if the background falls into shadow.

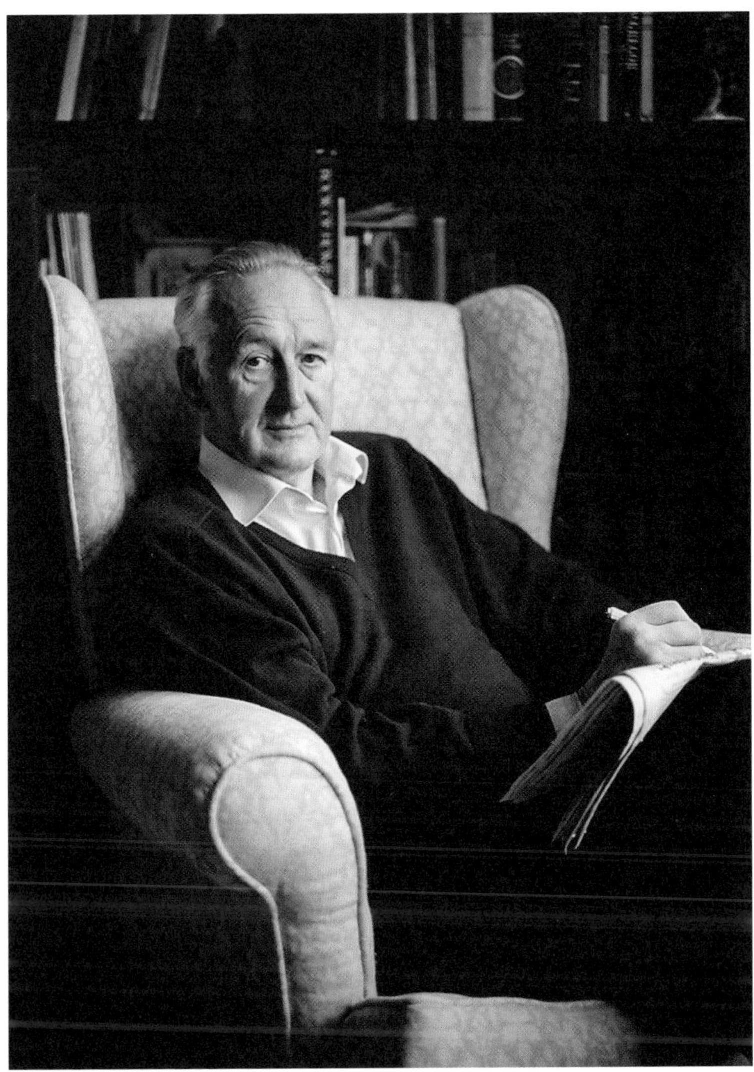

PRO TIPS

- Consider what's in the background: something relevant to your model will add context.
- Shoot with a fairly wide aperture, such as f/2, and focus on the eye nearest the camera.
- Don't worry if part of the face is in shadow. This can add depth and a little mystery to the shot. If you want to fill in some of the shadow, use a reflector, or get someone to hold up a piece of white card to bounce some of the light back onto the face.

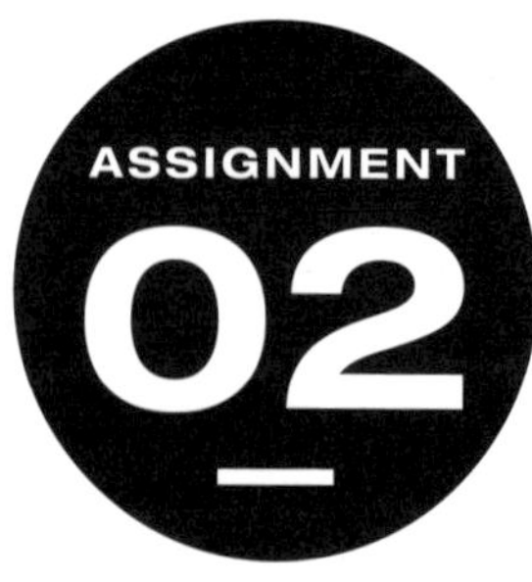

TECHNIQUE

- Shoot in Shutter Priority mode and experiment with different shutter speeds–somewhere between 1/15 and 1/125 sec. usually works well.
- Getting a good shot can be a bit "hit and miss," so shoot in Continuous mode to give yourself plenty of options.
- A mid-range aperture of around f/5.6 should work well but, if conditions are very bright, you could use a neutral density (ND) filter to prevent overexposure.
- Always "follow through" after you have clicked the shutter. This smooth and continuous action will help ensure a steady shot.
- Panning is easier if there's more distance between you and the subject, so consider using a longer lens.

▼ *Scenes with bold vertical lines in the background can give you a strong sense of motion.*

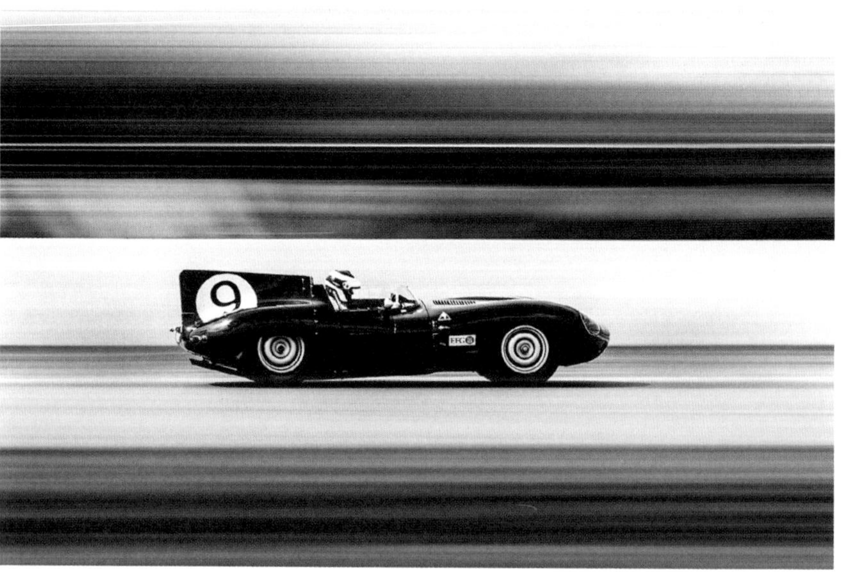

FAST TRACK

Panning can help you create the illusion of movement and speed in your images, and help to bring an otherwise "flat" black-and-white image to life. The idea of this technique is that the background is represented by a streaky blur, suggesting horizontal movement, while the main subject remains sharp, leading the viewer to think the subject is moving through the frame.

An effective but very simple concept, panning involves following a moving subject along the horizontal plane, using a slow shutter speed. The trick is to "keep up" with your subject so that it remains sharp, while the background becomes blurred.

To complete your assignment, try taking your camera along to a fast-moving sporting event, such as a motorsport, athletics, or cycling competition, or simply standing in the street. It's useful to choose a subject with predictable movement, which will make it easier to track, and the faster it's moving, the better. Your panned image could look great as a wide print, perhaps in 16:9 or even panoramic format.

PRO TIPS

- You'll need a steady hand and a stable stance as you follow the action. Plant your feet shoulder-width apart, press your elbows into your sides to help keep the camera on a level plane, rotate your torso to follow the action, and hit the shutter button as the subject passes in front of you. Alternatively, you could use a tripod with a panning head.
- Panning takes lots of practice, so don't give up if you're not getting the results you expect straight away.

ASSIGNMENT JOURNAL

TECHNIQUE

- Select a small aperture (ideally f/8 or smaller) to maximize depth of field and ensure the "real" and the reflected elements are all sharp.
- Capturing a good reflection often comes down to getting the right angle, so be prepared to experiment with different perspectives.
- Try to keep the sun out of your composition, as this could ruin your shot.

PRO TIPS

- Don't use a polarizing filter, as it will kill any reflections.
- Take care not to include yourself in the reflection (unless it's intentional).
- Keep your eyes open and look at every reflective surface. Opportunities arise when you least expect them to and often from the unlikeliest of sources.

JUST AN ILLUSION

Reflections are everywhere. From windows and puddles to shiny cars and buildings, there's usually a reflective surface of some kind close by, waiting to be photographed. Although beautiful and dramatic in their own right, this assignment is all about using reflections to create an illusion.

When we're shooting in black and white, rather than color, we need to make sure the content of our frame is easily recognizable. So, try to aim for distinct shapes with a strong separation between tones. To create your illusion, consider using architectural reflections (building windows, for example), environmental reflections (particularly waterscapes, such as ponds and lakes), or abstract reflections (the surface of a clean car, perhaps).

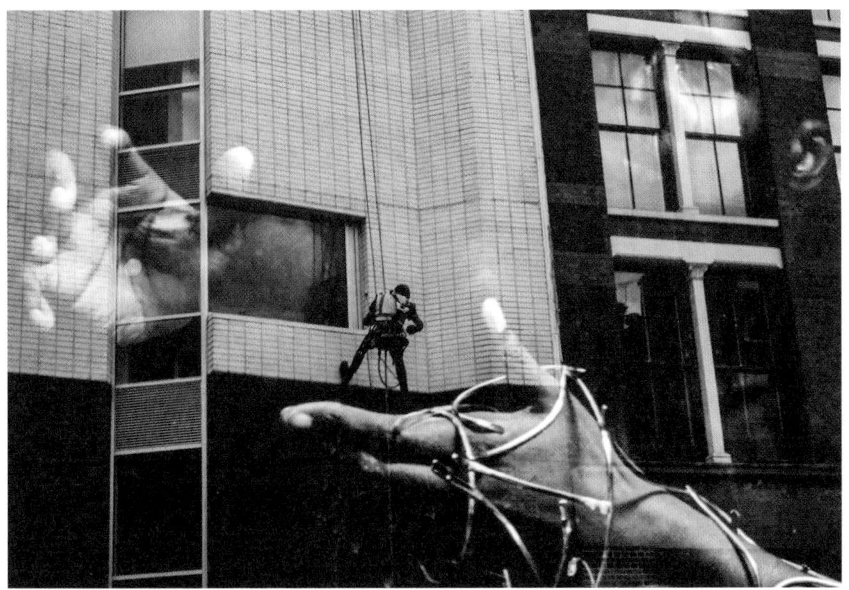

▲ *You can use reflections to play tricks with the mind and create an alternative version of reality.*

▼ *Huge windows can distort the reality of a reflected image. In this case, the reflected buildings have a wavy appearance.*

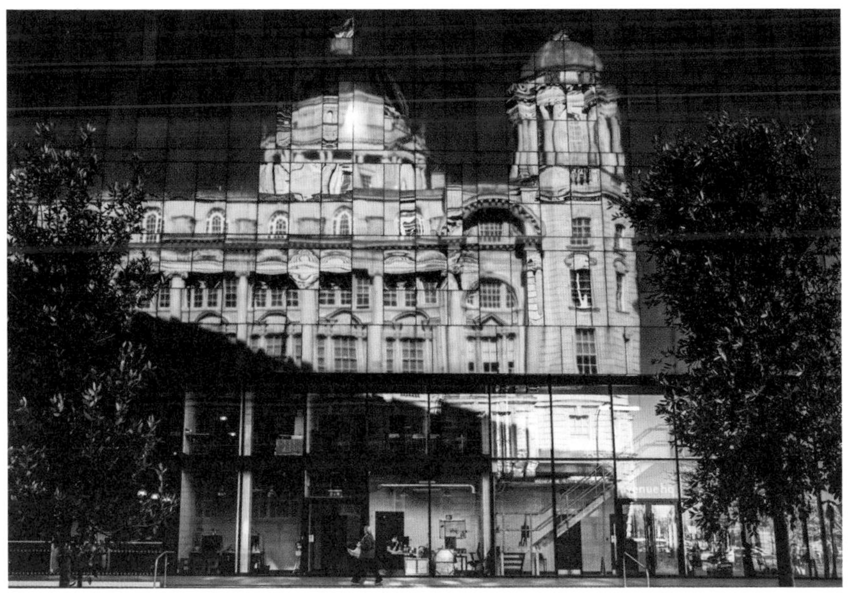

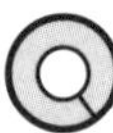

TECHNIQUE

- Shoot close-up. While you probably won't need a macro lens, you'll still need to isolate the detail, so a medium telephoto zoom will be ideal.
- As well as shooting similar subject matter, take a uniform approach to lighting, composition, and editing. This will give your images a cohesive and consistent feel.
- If you're shooting interior detail, try shooting through the car windows and including some reflection on the glass.
- You'll probably be shooting some highly reflective surfaces, so use available light (and a tripod, if necessary). Also, experiment with shooting angles to make the best of the light.
- Aim for high contrast, with punchy blacks and bright whites, to emphasize the detail.

▼ *Try using a wide aperture to throw the background out of focus and create something stylized and distinctive.*

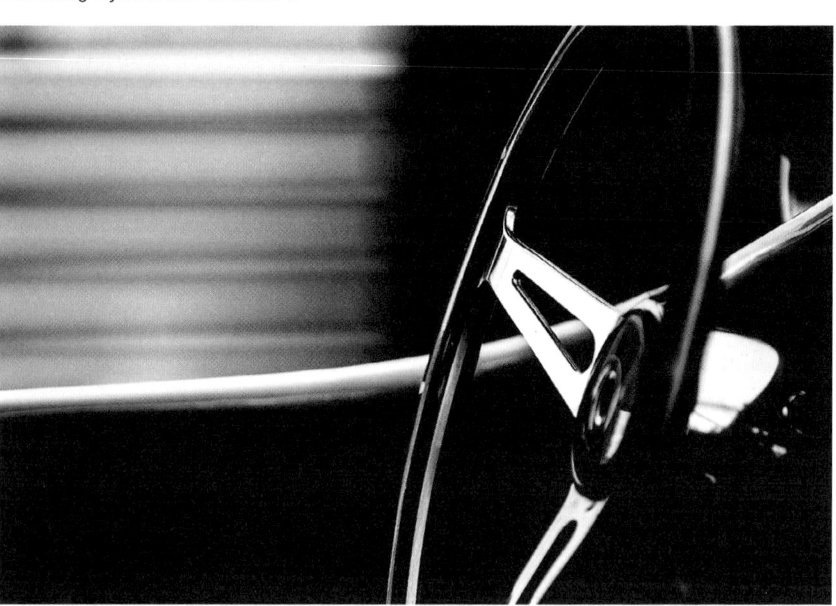

SHIFTING GEARS

The automotive world can be a very photogenic one and is perhaps underrepresented when it comes to black-and-white imagery. This assignment isn't so much about shooting cars themselves, but more about capturing their detail. Whether it's engine parts, shiny chrome features, vintage dashboard instruments, or smart alloy wheels, the small detail can give you plenty of opportunity to practice your close-up skills and create engaging images.

Certain car brands and models are known for their distinctive or quirky features–the Rolls-Royce Spirit of Ecstasy ornament, for example, or the chrome gear lever gate in an old Ferrari. It's good to include elements such as these to make the subject more identifiable.

This could make a great wall-art project, perhaps with 12 small, framed images displayed together as a grid. However, rather than having a random collection of car parts, try to keep your project focused. To do this, you could photograph one brand or model throughout the project; shoot cars of a specific genre or from a particular era; choose to capture similar objects from different cars; or give your images an abstract feel by using reflections, contours, or lines.

▼ *Using available light, rather than artifical, helps prevent unwanted glare and can give you a more atmospheric result.*

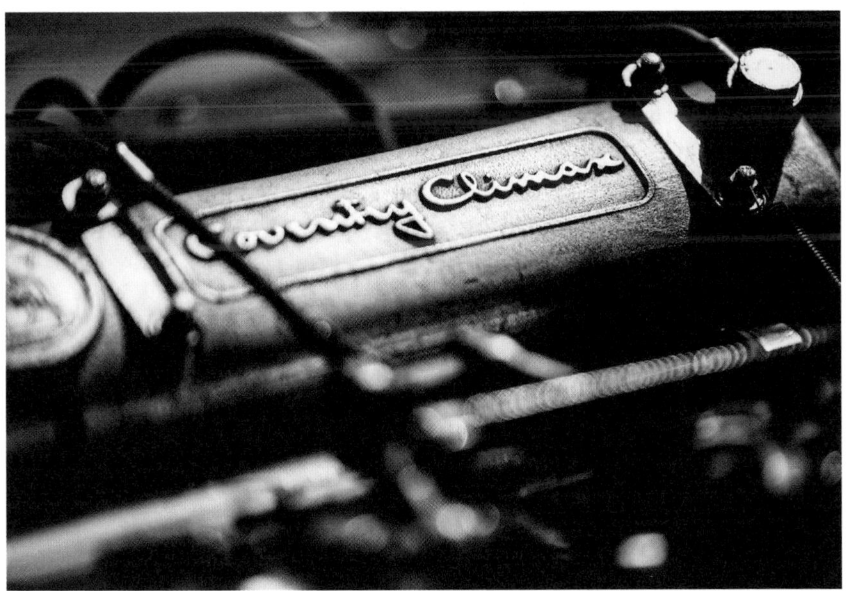

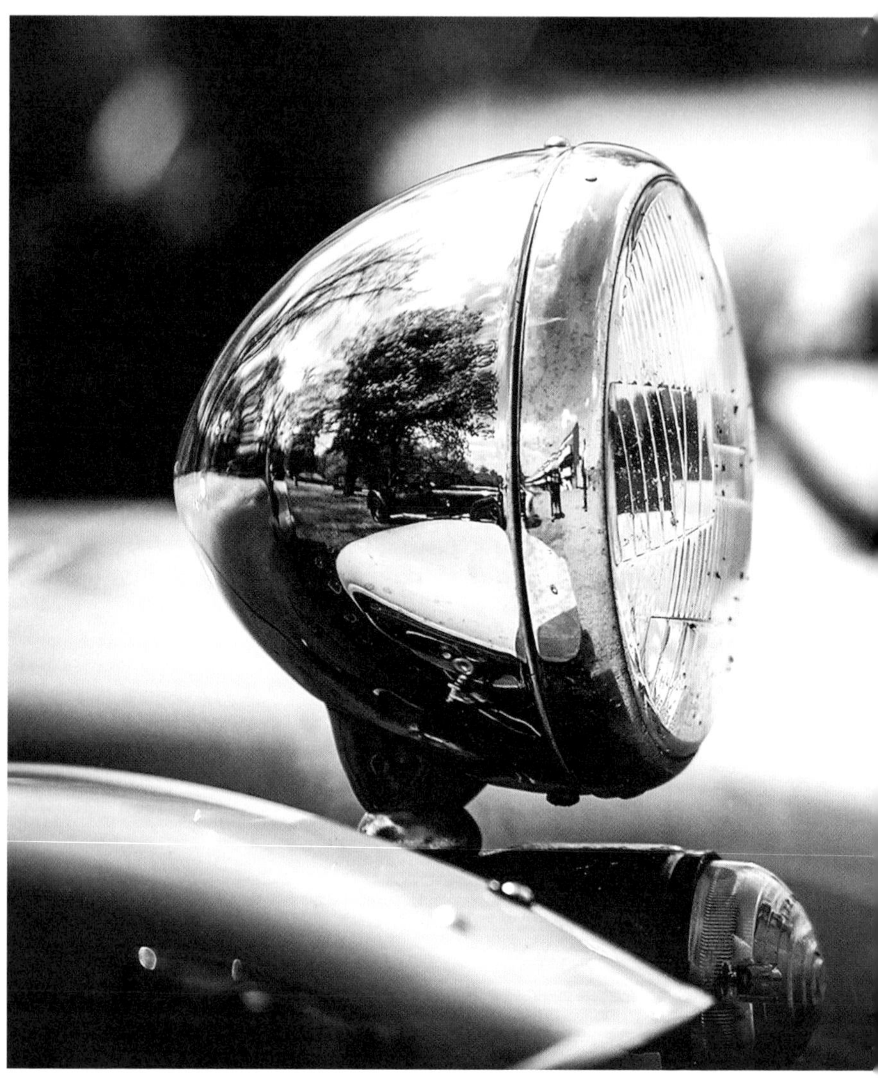

ASSIGNMENT JOURNAL

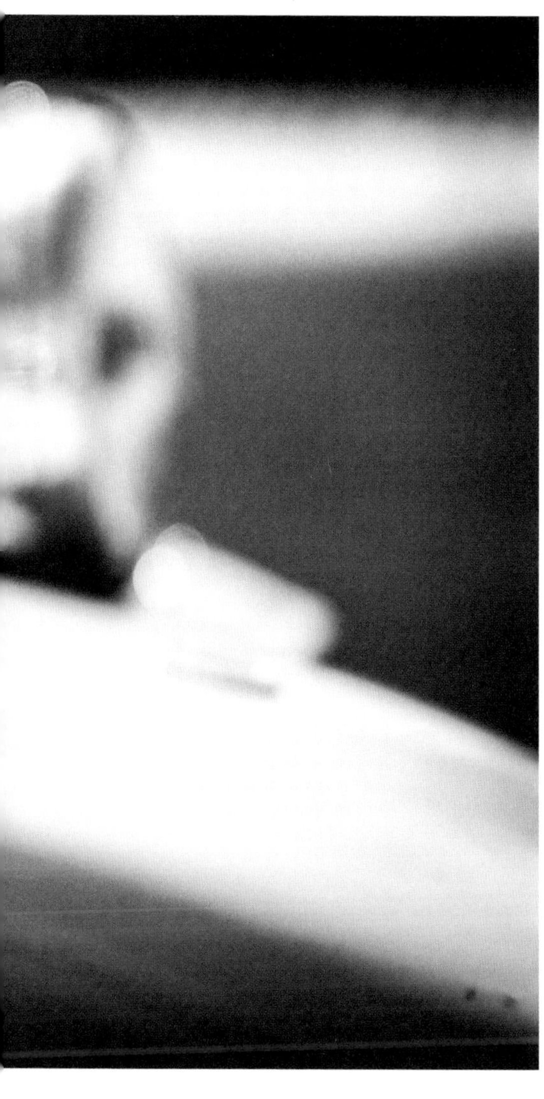

PRO TIPS

- Take care when shooting chrome: make sure it's clean and avoid capturing any unwanted reflections, including your own.
- Visit car shows, race days, car part sales, and other automotive events–you'll find plenty of inspiration and an abundance of subject matter.
- You could treat this as a long-term project, and even produce a photobook once you have enough images.

◀ *There are lots of opportunities for shots like this at classic car shows and events.*

TECHNIQUE

- When choosing a lens, always take into account your camera's crop factor. For example, a 35mm lens with a 1.5x crop sensor would be equivalent to approximately 50mm in full-frame terms.
- To find the "sweet spot" of your lens, attach a newspaper page (ideally, a page with very small print) to the wall, set your camera on a tripod a few feet away, then photograph the page at every aperture. The "sweet spot" is the frame that has the best edge-to-edge sharpness.
- Try some low-light shooting with your 50mm lens. The combination of its low weight and fast maximum aperture will help you get sharp images without too much noise.

ASSIGNMENT JOURNAL

PRO TIPS

- This lens is ideal for isolating detail in close-up (though not usually macro), when the lens is wide open.
- Vintage lenses may have imperfections–notably, being soft at the edges when wide open–but this often adds character and a pleasing eccentricity.
- Consider buying an older 50mm manual focus lens from a second-hand store or auction site. They tend to be very cheap, though in some cases you may need an adapter.

NIFTY FIFTY

Anyone who took up photography between the 1950s and 1990s will be familiar with the humble 50mm "standard" lens. This is a prime lens with a focal length roughly equivalent to the diagonal measurement of the sensor (or film). Once the staple lens of the amateur photographer, the "nifty fifty" is now often overlooked, but, in this assignment, you'll be bringing it back to life.

Imposing constraints can be a great way to improve skills and encourage creativity, and that's exactly what this assignment is all about: getting creative with just one "ordinary" lens. Choose a period (ideally a whole week) when you'll be doing lots of shooting and restrict yourself to the 50mm lens (or its equivalent). Resist the temptation to try other lenses and get used to this lens—work out its "sweet spot" (see Technique) and its limits, and understand how it "describes" the world. This exercise can help sharpen your compositional skills and make you more instinctive, which is particularly great for street or travel photography.

▼ *The 50mm lens can be great for shooting portraits, providing a flattering, natural look with a neutral perspective.*

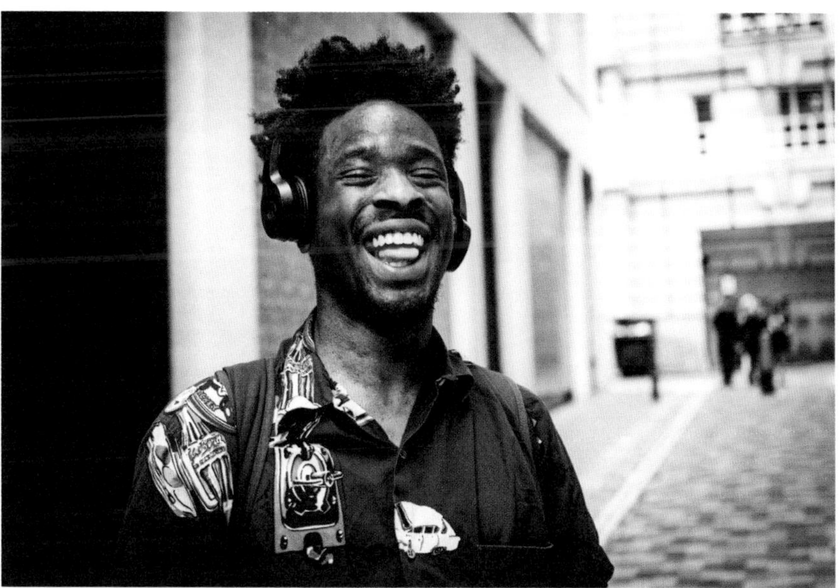

TECHNIQUE

- The wider the angles, the stronger the dynamic tension will be. The widest angle possible between two intersecting diagonals is 90°, so a good way to introduce dynamic tension is to include paths that intersect at this angle.
- Try to visualize diagonal lines and triangles in the scenes around you, as these tend to jar with our natural sense of balance.
- Consider using strong diagonals to dissect a picture, dividing it up into two contradictory stories.

FEEL THE TENSION

Dynamic tension uses the energy in an image to draw the eye out of the frame and in opposite directions. It creates a small visual shock and a degree of discomfort, making the viewer sit up and take notice. In a way, it's a contradiction to the leading lines rule.

Imagine a person standing on a perfectly horizontal line. If you change the angle of that line to 30°, for example, the person will look unbalanced and disorientated. This is dynamic tension.

For this assignment, try to find an instance of dynamic tension and create an image that has an inherent sense of unease. This is an exercise in "seeing" and trying to spot the possibilities in a scene. To give your image a sense of discord, look out for diagonal lines moving away from each other in different directions; triangular shapes, either naturally occurring or implied in your composition; and contrasting body language between two or more people.

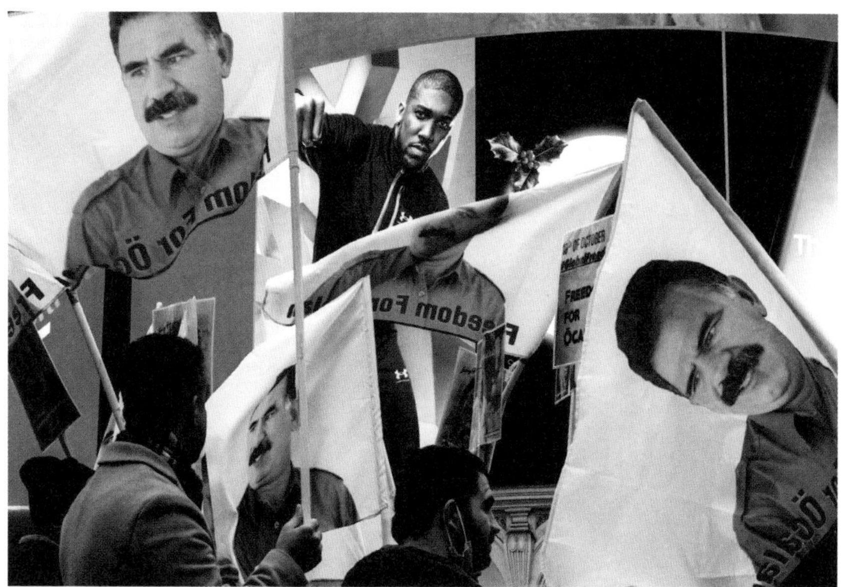

▲ *Here, dynamic tension is induced by the heads all facing in different directions. It's slightly confusing to look at but somehow you're drawn in.*

PRO TIPS

- You can use angles, particularly diagonals, to subtly change the mood of an image and induce feelings such as calmness, anger, or aggression.
- Try tilting the camera at varying angles to put your subject on a slant. (Known as the "Dutch tilt" or "Dutch angle," this technique is often overused, so employ sparingly!)
- Try to imagine things "sliding off" your diagonal lines, heading outward, toward the edges of the frame. When that's happening, you know you've got tension.

ASSIGNMENT JOURNAL

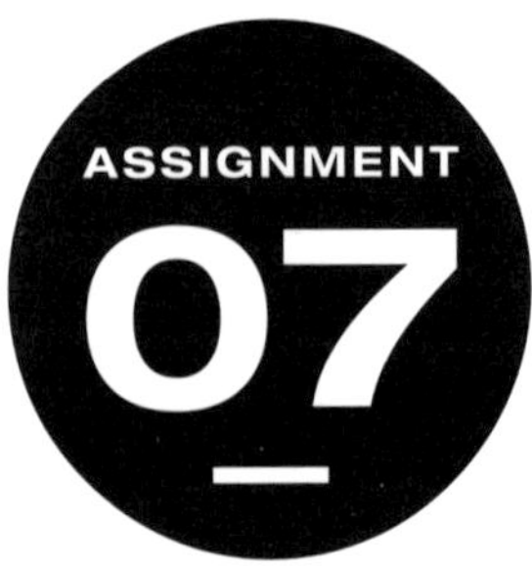

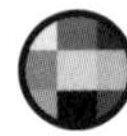

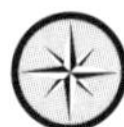

TECHNIQUE

- As the sky will be the key component in the frame, use a wideangle lens to ensure you capture a big expanse of it in your shot.
- Being ready and in position is everything: a sunrise can happen very quickly and changes in the light are rapid, so make sure you're in the right place at the right time.
- Use a tripod so that you can use a slower shutter speed (1/15 to 1/30 sec. is ideal) and maximize the potential of a low ISO.

PRO TIPS

- Be an early bird! The most dramatic moments often happen before you expect them to. Plan to be in position 20–30 minutes before the official sunrise time.
- Experiment with lots of different combinations of color adjustments in post-processing.
- Use an app, such as PhotoPills, to help you get the perfect position and timing.

ASSIGNMENT JOURNAL

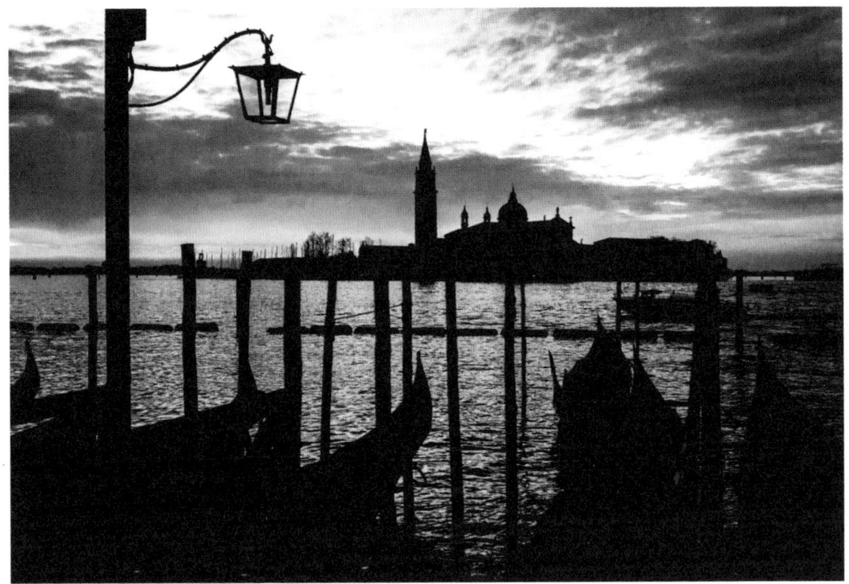

▲ *The gradation in the sky's tones can be easily achieved by tweaking the color sliders in post-processing.*

RISE AND SHINE

We might be used to seeing photographs of sunrises in amazing yellow, orange, red, magenta, and blue hues, but that doesn't mean we should overlook the possibility of shooting them in monochrome.

Great black-and-white photographers are able to pre-visualize how colors will look in a monochromatic image. This is a skill we all need to develop and will be key to this assignment, which focuses on how to express colors in a range of gray tones.

Your brief here is to take a photograph of a sunrise. At this time of day, the sky contains a wide range of strong hues. To get the best out of these colors, shoot in Raw and make fine adjustments to the color channels later in post-processing.

TECHNIQUE

- Set your ISO to 400 and the aperture to f/8. In good light you should have a shutter speed fast enough to freeze any movement and get a sharp image.
- High-contrast images work well when there is a clear separation between the subject and the background.
- Timing is key: always be ready, with your camera in your hand, switched on and pre-set, with the lens cap off.

HONORING HENRI

Henri Cartier-Bresson is considered to be the great-grandfather of street photography and is well known for coming up with the concept of the decisive moment—that split second when the visual and psychological elements of people in a street scene spontaneously and briefly come together in perfect harmony to convey the essence of that situation.

Shooting in black and white, usually on a Leica rangefinder camera with a 50mm lens, Cartier-Bresson relished this fleeting and very transitory moment which, for many street shooters, is the very essence of street photography. This is something we can all do and your aim here is to capture a decisive moment.

Your image should be candid, but you can watch and wait as a scenario unfolds and take a number of shots. To add authenticity to the assignment, try to put yourself in HC-B's shoes and shoot with his technical limitations, using a 50mm lens and an ISO no faster than 400.

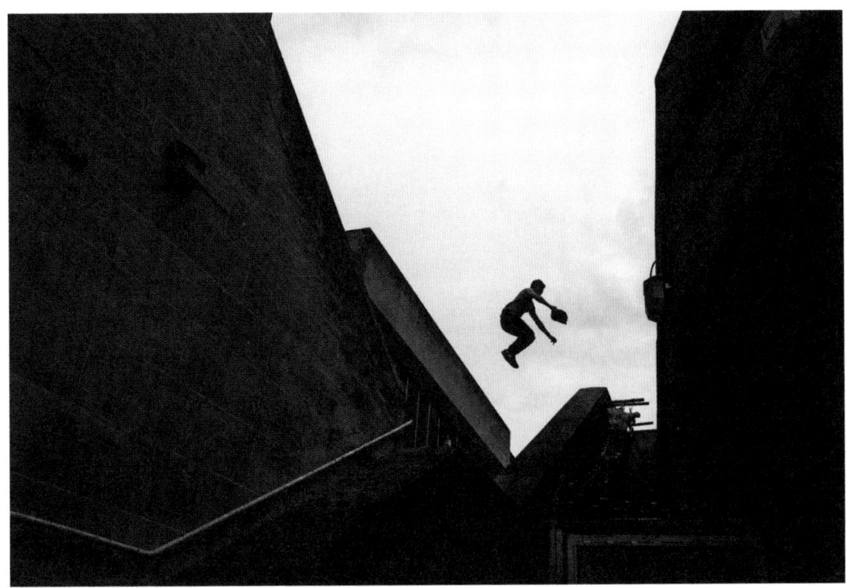

▲ *Occasionally, you'll get lucky and be in the right place at the right time. If you're going to capture scenes like this, you (and your camera) need to be in "always on" mode.*

PRO TIPS

- Take lots of frames and try shooting in Continuous mode.
- Don't worry about "perfection"—study some of HC-B's work and you'll see that much of it is far from perfect.
- Don't give up too quickly! There's a lot of luck involved when trying to create this kind of shot, so be patient.
- Try shooting on (fast) film to really get into the spirit of this assignment.

ASSIGNMENT JOURNAL

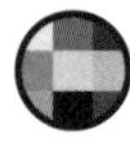

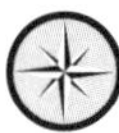

TECHNIQUE

- Before you set out with your camera, make a list of all the things that have a strong local identity. For example, if you were visiting Lisbon in Portugal, your list could include trams, cobbles, sardines, fado bars, pastéis de nata, Vasco da Gama Bridge, and so on.
- Make your list as comprehensive as possible and try to include things like people, buildings, transport, the weather, the landscape, food and drink, landmarks, and souvenirs.
- Aim to shoot a multi-layered image with the "local context" acting as one of the layers, typically the foreground, middle ground, or background.

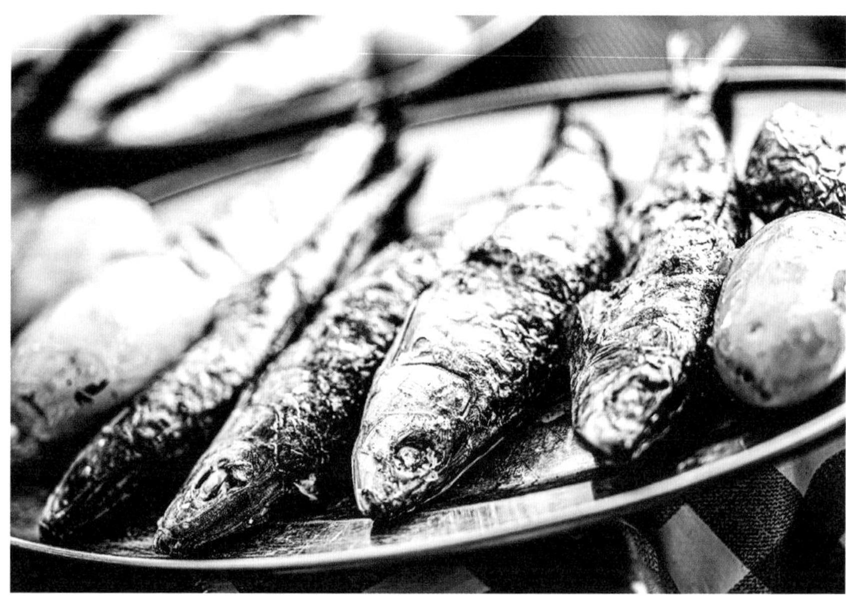

A SENSE OF PLACE

Let's face it, most travel photographs are shot in color, but that doesn't mean to say they can't be shot in black and white—we just have to work that little bit harder to make our images interesting, informative, and engaging for the viewer.

We often hear about the importance of "storytelling" in travel photography, but we don't always see much evidence of it—and that's because it's quite difficult to achieve. This assignment will help give your images a strong narrative, together with that crucial sense of place.

There is a simple but effective method of making connections you can use, which will ensure your images go beyond the "obvious" shots of touristic locations. Take a street market, for example—one market looks pretty much like another, but if your photograph includes some local fish that is only caught in that area, the image immediately conveys a sense of place.

So, the idea here is to compile a list of items that are significant to the area, then consciously incorporate one of them into every shot—and bingo! You have now achieved that sense of place, as well as incorporating a strong storyline. When viewed as a collection, your images will feel much more connected, which is particularly important if you plan to produce a photobook, for instance.

PRO TIPS

- Good travel photography is all about observation, so walk slowly and look for fragments of local detail.
- Be flexible with your list, adding to it as you discover new things.
- If you intend to shoot in black and white on your travels, be committed to that medium and don't succumb to color—you won't regret it!

◀ No photo essay about Lisbon in Portugal would be complete without at least one picture of sardines.

ASSIGNMENT JOURNAL

TECHNIQUE

- Aim for a single point of interest, rather than multiple focal points. You want the viewer's eye to study form, not content.
- In terms of exposure, a "contrasty" image with big, deep blacks and crisp whites often works well. You might be able to make these tweaks in post-processing, particularly if you're shooting in Raw.
- Spot metering can help you expose the most important part of the frame correctly.
- Try at least one minimalist shot using shadows alone. You'll be surprised at how effective this can be.

LESS IS MORE

You can't beat a bit of minimalism when it comes to black-and-white photography—the medium was made for it. The ability to reduce a subject to a very simplified form is not always as easy as it looks, but, once you've got the hang of pre-visualizing the result, you'll be creating some striking pieces of contemporary art, which is the goal of this assignment.

Your brief here is to find a subject with minimal clutter and distracting material. You should aim for simple shapes and a strong contrast between dark and light tones. Your subject could be a landscape, still life, street scene, person, something abstract, or even just shadows. Before taking the photograph, try to imagine what the finished result would look like as a large print on your wall.

◀ *In this shot, the brightness of the snow masked out any distracting background detail.*

PRO TIPS

- If your camera allows it, this is a good time to set your viewfinder to monochrome so that you'll have a better idea of what the finished image will look like.
- Bear in mind that ambiguity is a good quality in minimalism, leaving the viewer to make up their own story about what the image contains.
- Don't be afraid of using negative space (and particularly white space) to enhance the minimalist effect and create feelings of isolation.

TECHNIQUE

- You'll need lots of patience. Be prepared to wait for the "perfect" scene to evolve.
- Beware of converging verticals (when two parallel lines appear to get closer) and use your image-editing software to straighten up the lines of buildings.
- Bear in mind that the "feel" of a corner will change throughout the day and at different times of the year. You may need to make several visits to get the shots you want.

ASSIGNMENT JOURNAL

PRO TIPS

- If you visit a corner that you think has potential but it doesn't work out, try again on a different day. Corner scenes are constantly changing!
- Don't overlook the possibility of producing some fine-art prints for this project—corners can be very photogenic places. You could even ask a local coffee shop to display a small exhibition of your framed prints.

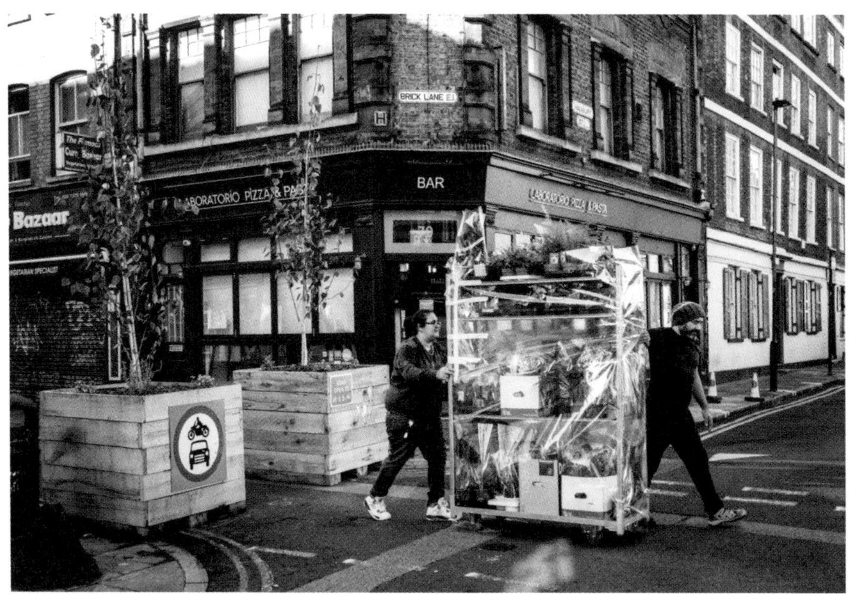

▲ *There's often activity at these intersections and sometimes it's worth hanging around to see what's going to happen.*

GET CORNERED

There's something about the geometry of street corners that makes them fascinating places, but there's more to it than that. For the photographer, street corners represent a constant state of flux, a place where worlds collide and where lives intersect each other. In other words, where there's a corner, there's life.

In this assignment, you'll create a small project (perhaps aim to produce a set of six or eight prints) based on corners. Your project could be based on the buildings themselves, without people, or it could reflect the bustle and ever-changing life at these intersections.

Decide on a consistent theme for your collection of images. You could choose to shoot corners in one geographical area or corners that are similar in some way. Or, you could choose to photograph a range of corners, using a particular style. Whatever theme you choose, this visual "glue" will help to hold the images together as a cohesive project.

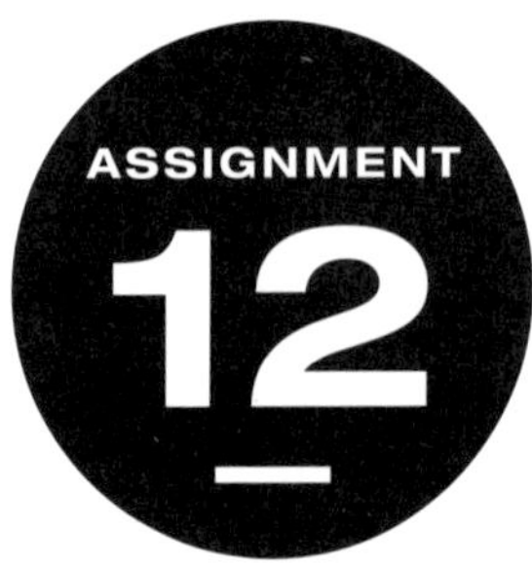

TECHNIQUE

- Choose a Raw image with an even range of tones, possibly one that you feel is a little lifeless.
- Don't go over the top with the effects—there's a fine line between subtle enhancement and overkill.

PRO TIPS

- If you don't shoot in Raw, you can achieve similar effects with a Jpeg, as long as your software has a Camera Raw Filter. (In Adobe Photoshop, you can access this by pressing Shift+Command+A.)

▼ *Before: The image is quite "flat" and lacks tonality and depth.*

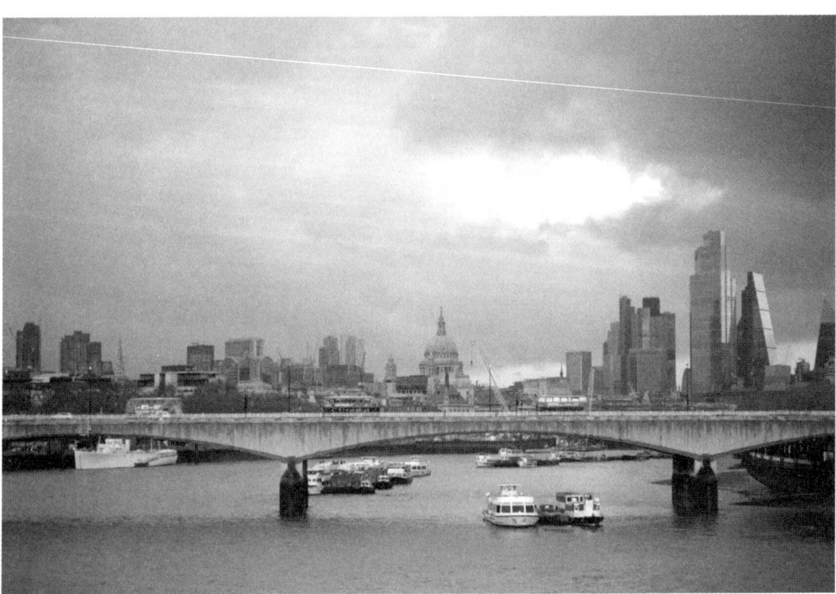

BALANCING ACT

If you're a traditional printer, the concept of tonal balance will be very familiar to you, but, for most of us, it's a skill we need to develop. In the darkroom, the tonal balance of a black-and-white frame would be achieved by printing some areas lighter or darker, accentuating certain sections of the image and making others less prominent. This process is often referred to as "dodging and burning" (lightening and darkening).

Black-and-white images sometimes appear "flat" and lack punch. Your assignment is to take an image and, with the subtle use of light and color in post-processing, improve the tonal balance of the photograph, providing a wider range of tones. This can be done easily, without the complexity of adjustment layers, using this very simple method (below).

THE PROCESS

1 Convert your Raw file to black and white.

2 Enhance the tonality by tweaking the color channels in your editing software. For example, in the "after" image (overleaf), these changes were made:

- Increased the values on the orange and yellow Saturation sliders to emphasize the bridge (a similar effect to dodging, but more targeted).
- Increased the value on the blue Saturation slider to selectively darken the sky.
- Increased the value on the red Saturation slider to make the buses a little more obvious.

3 Open the file as a Jpeg and make final adjustments to light and shade using the Brush Tool (dodging and burning).

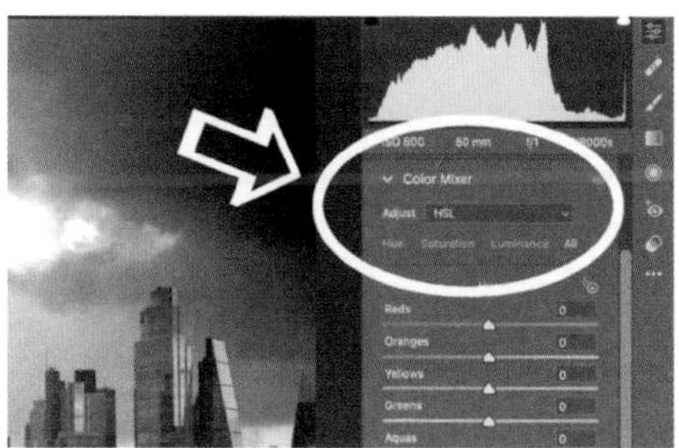

▲ *You'll find the Color Mixer sliders in the control panel of your editing software.*

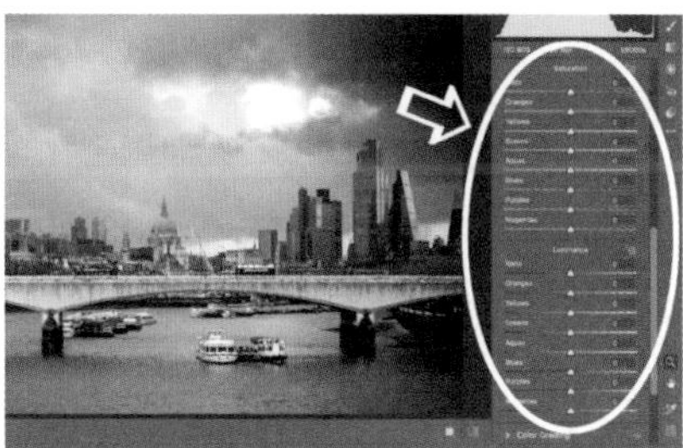

▲ *Open up the Color Mixer panel and you'll find sliders to adjust hue, saturation, and luminance. Experiment with these until you get the desired effect.*

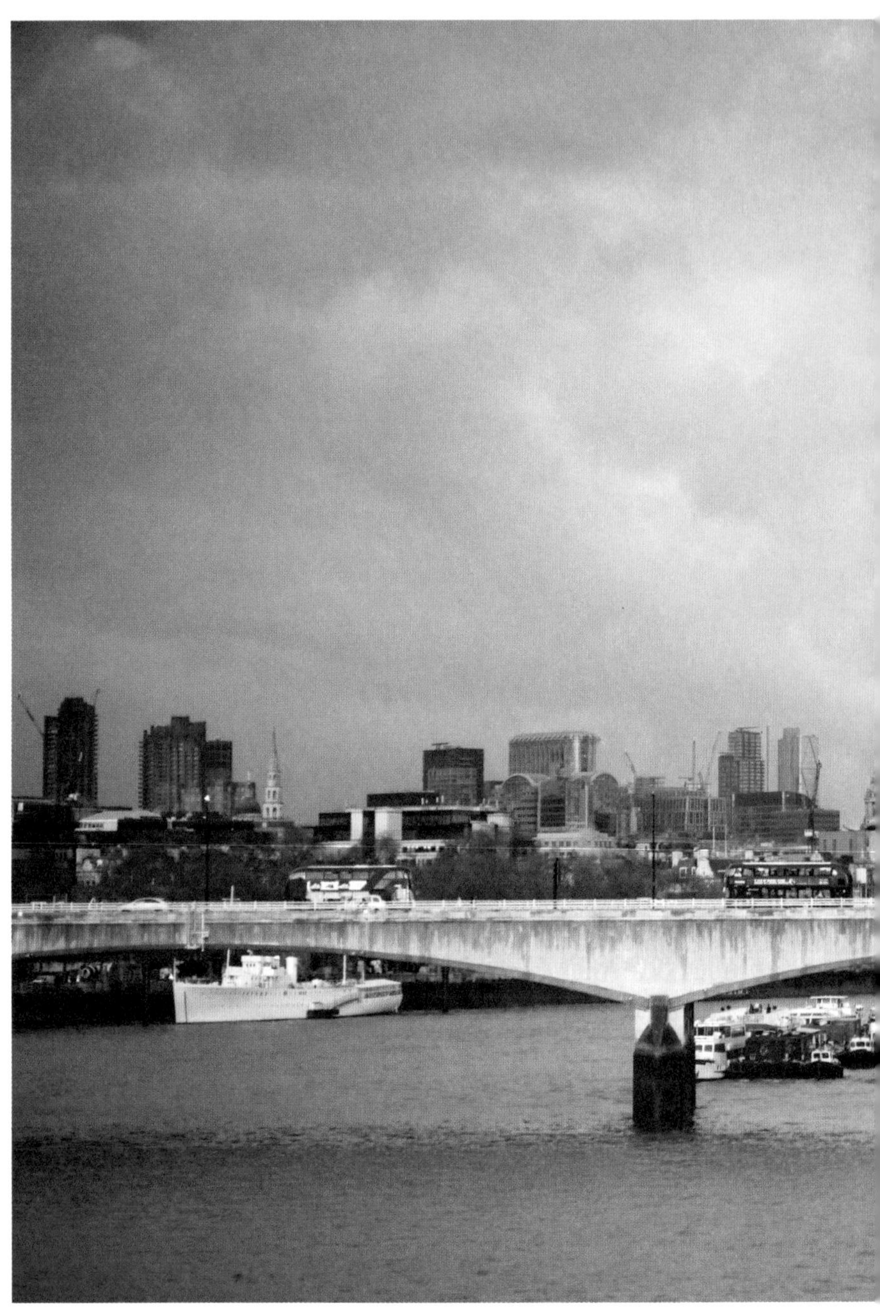

▲ *After: With some subtle changes to contrast and tweaks to the saturation on the color sliders, the image has more punch and a greater range of tones.*

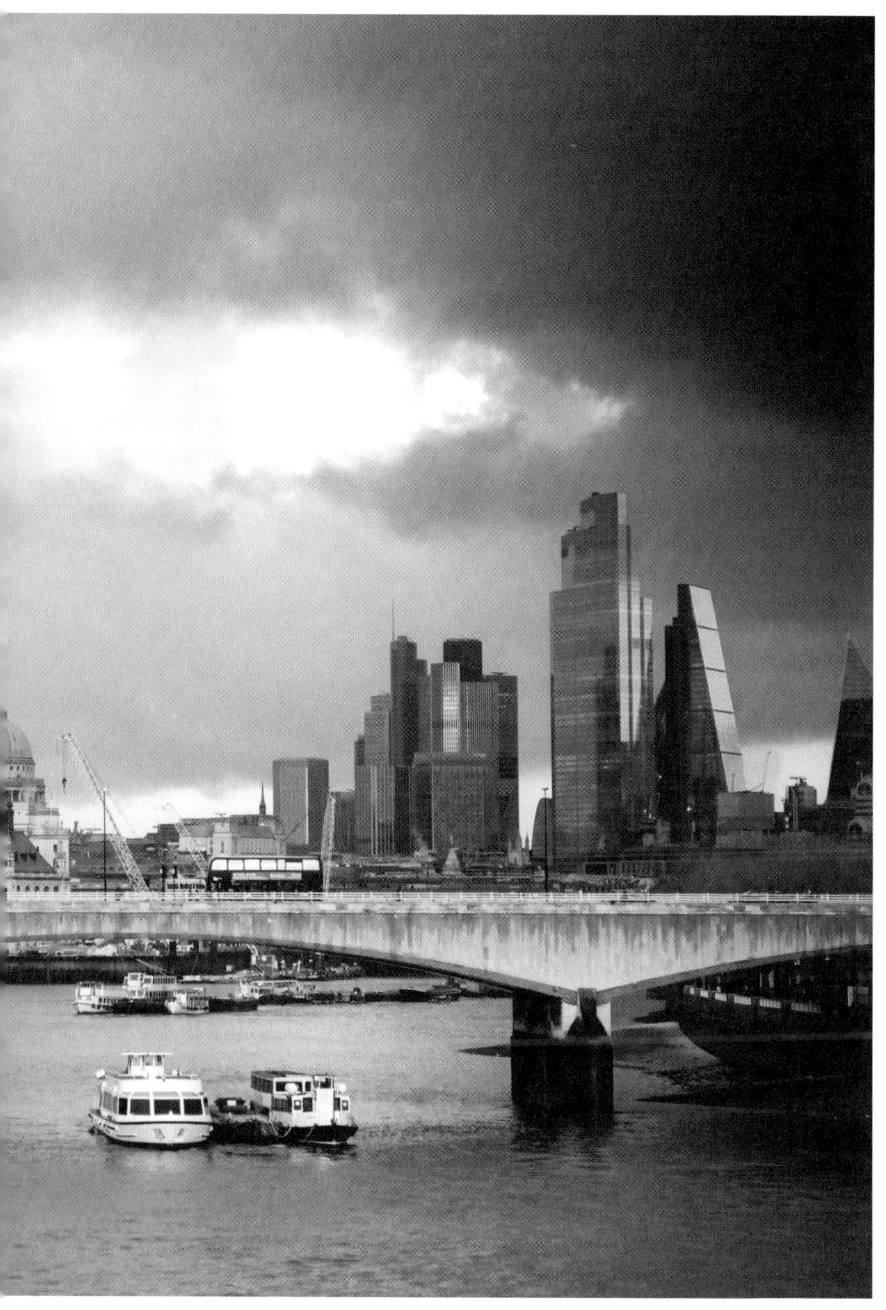

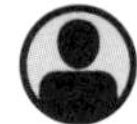

TECHNIQUE

- Use a tripod and remote release (or your camera's self-timer).
- Lighting is important and will set the tone for how your personality is conveyed.
- Take some cues from the art world by finding some self-portraits that inspire you.

REINVENT YOUR SELFIE

The world is obsessed with taking pictures of themselves and the "selfie" is part of the zeitgeist of the 21st century. But self-portraits have been around for much longer than that, and they are a legitimate art form in themselves. As photographers, we should all have a good selfie that we can use on our social media profiles or websites, or just for fun.

For this assignment, you are going to create a selfie. Black-and-white self-portraits seem to have more gravitas than color ones. They tend to look more elegant, more stylish, and more confident. But where do you start?

The first consideration is how you want to come across. Do you want your image to be serious or a little playful? Do you want to include a background or some props that are relevant to you? Will you use the image in a business context? Work out what you want it to say, then go for it with real intent.

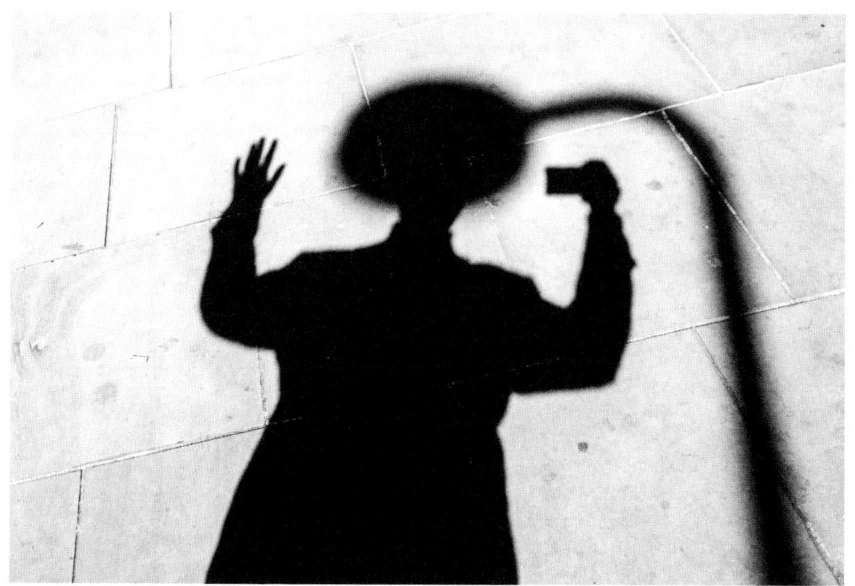

▲ *Something fun like this shot can be great for social media profiles, especially if you want to be anonymous!*

PRO TIPS

Here are ten variations to try, none of them requiring professional lighting and all very easy to do:

- Silhouette—this can say as much about you as a fully lit shot.
- Reflection—shoot yourself using a mirror or any shiny surface.
- Motion blur—set a slow shutter speed and move during the exposure for something really creative.
- Partial reveal—try cutting the face vertically and only shooting half of it.
- Extreme close-up—shoot just your favorite facial feature and leave the viewer guessing about the rest.
- Triptych—use three images side by side to tell a mini story about you.
- Angles—shun eye-level shooting for something more quirky and dramatic.
- Low lighting—dark contrast selfies can be very powerful.
- Context—shoot yourself holding your favorite camera, or in your car or work environment.
- Multiple exposure—why not create more than one of you?

TECHNIQUE

- Approach people from the front or side, rather than from the back, which could appear threatening.
- A focal length of around 85mm is perfect, and try the widest aperture for a less distracting background.
- Scout around for great light and don't be afraid to move someone into more flattering light.
- It will be tempting to get it over with quickly, but don't rush—you need to make the most of the situation. Most subjects will be happy to spend a few minutes with you.
- Don't be afraid to direct your subjects. People generally feel more comfortable if someone else is in control.

PRO TIPS

- Consider having an instant camera with you. It takes a few seconds to take an extra shot and you'll find that most people love getting that little print in their hands.
- Be generous: offer to send the subject a copy of the image. It's a nice quid pro quo for their time and attention.
- Have some business cards made to hand out to people you approach. This will help make you feel more confident and appear "legitimate."

ASSIGNMENT JOURNAL

► *Many people feel more comfortable if you ask them to carry on with what they were doing, rather than to pose for you.*

TOTAL STRANGER

How many times, when you're walking the streets, do you see someone who looks interesting, think about asking them for a picture, but then back out? Many of us find the idea of approaching a stranger awkward or intimidating, but it needn't be—and it's actually much easier than you think.

Walking up to someone and asking to take their picture will be difficult at first, but you'll find that you get used to it very quickly. And you'll also find that most people are receptive and usually flattered to be asked. Do mention to them that you're shooting in black and white—many will find this intriguing and you'll come across as someone who knows what they're doing!

Before you venture out to complete this assignment, think about your approach. As you walk over to the person, you should smile and raise your camera slightly so that your intentions are clear—don't try to hide your camera, as this could make you look shifty. You'll need to be confident and well-practiced, knowing how you're going to introduce yourself. Work out a script and be prepared to explain what you're doing. Keep it short and snappy—this isn't the time for your life story.

Rejection is all part of the game—part of the fun, even. Take it on the chin. You'll almost certainly find that you have a "yes" rate of around 80–90 percent, but if someone says "no," that's no problem—just move on to the next one.

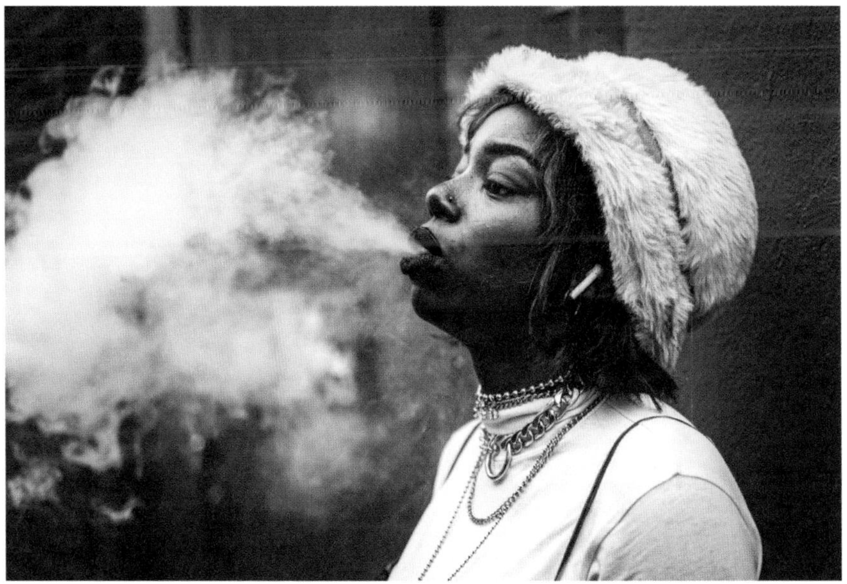

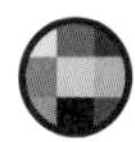

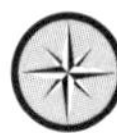
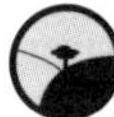

TECHNIQUE

- Take care with the highlights if the clouds are very bright. You want to avoid blown-out highlights, so make sure you keep an eye on your histogram.
- Contrast is your friend: you need light clouds with a dark sky or dark clouds with a light sky. Filters can help you emphasize the desired effect.
- Cloudscapes can change rapidly, so you may need to wait to get the perfect formation for your shot.
- You'll often find clouds looking most dramatic at dawn and dusk, so be prepared to put in some long hours!

LONELY AS A CLOUD

Often considered as the "drug of choice" for many landscape photographers, clouds are a really good way of setting the mood in a photograph. Light, fluffy clouds against a pale blue sky can induce feelings of springtime and happiness, while dark, threatening clouds will engender an angry mood.

The good news is that clouds can look great in black and white, so, your brief here is to compose a shot where clouds are the key feature in the frame, rather than a pretty addition to the background. The ideal weather conditions for this project will be blue skies with some cloud (50–70 percent cloud cover would be ideal).

This could be the time to reach for your filters. Depending on which filter you need, you can use physical filters on the front of the lens, in-camera digital filters, or filter effects added in post-processing. They will all give you similar effects. The three filters you'll find most useful for this assignment are: a red filter, to darken the blue sky and help to emphasize the clouds; a neutral density (ND) filter, to allow you to use a very slow shutter speed to show the ghostly swirls of scudding clouds (particularly good on a windy day when the clouds are moving quickly); and a graduated filter, to increase contrast in the upper part of the frame.

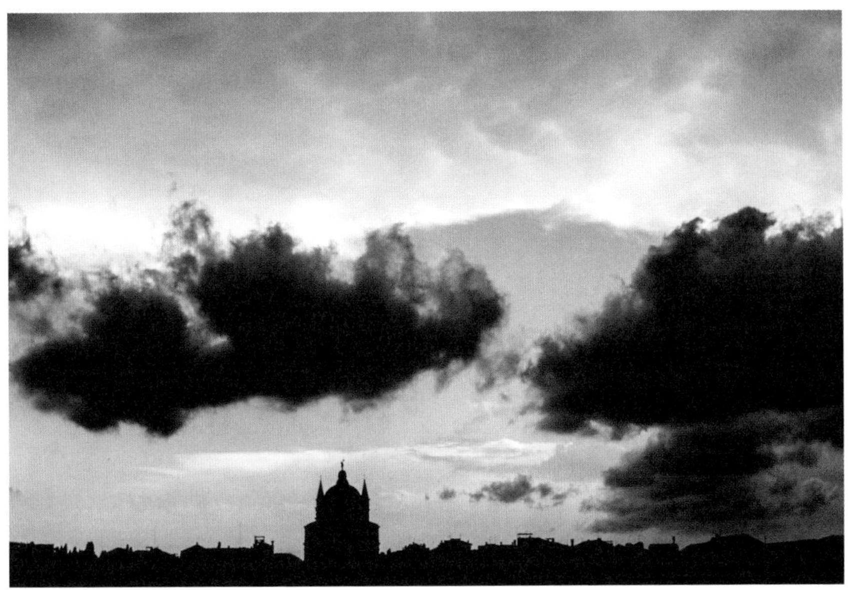

▲ *Clouds are not always white! In this case, the dark cloud structure sets a more oppressive, angry tone.*

▼ *You could try something more abstract. The reflection of the clouds is the key feature in this urban landscape.*

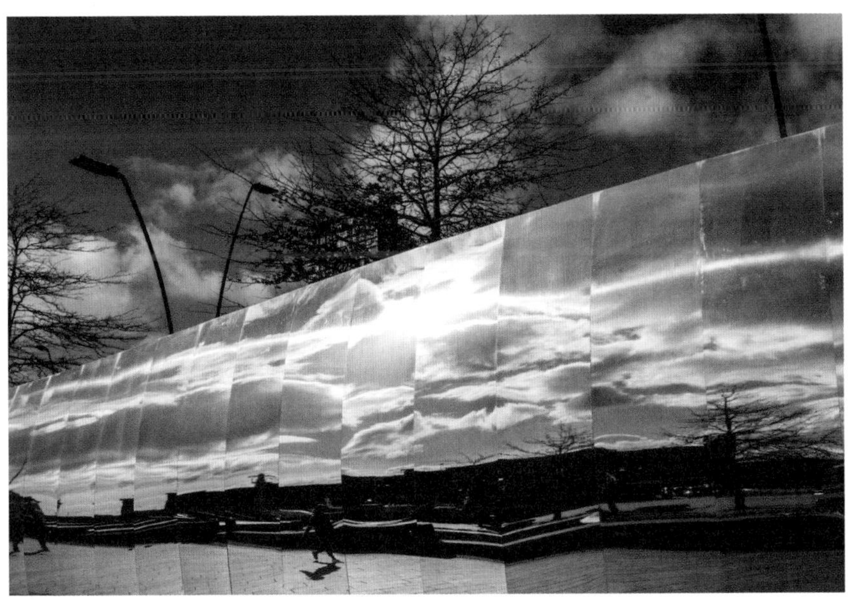

TECHNIQUE

- A wideangle prime lens (28–35mm) is ideal for urban landscapes. Use a tilt-shift lens (or post-processing software) to correct converging verticals and straighten up tall buildings.
- Plan ahead and choose the time of day carefully. The quality and angle of the light can make or break any shot, and this is especially true for urban landscape photography. A subject that looks dull and uninspiring at one time of day can transform into a truly spellbinding image just with the passing of a few hours.
- Experiment with different viewpoints to find the most interesting perspective.

▼ *It's useful to use elements in the scene to frame the individual, as the deep shadows are doing here.*

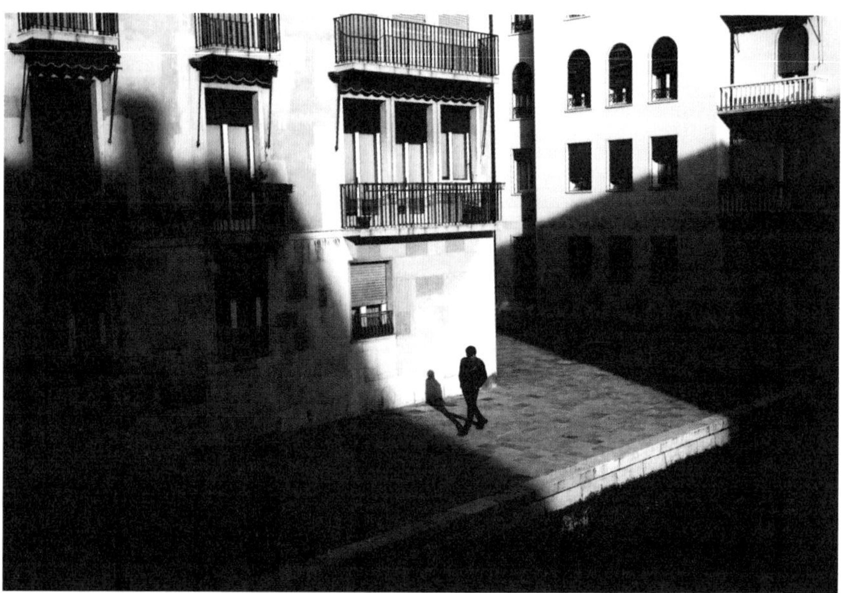

URBAN LIVING

In this project, you'll blend cityscape, architectural, and street photography to document the relationship between humans and the built environment. Although urban landscapes can be shot devoid of people, some element of humanity can add a sense of realism, bringing life to an otherwise "dead" scene.

Your assignment is to shoot an urban landscape that contains at least one person to "anchor" your composition and introduce an impression of scale, perspective, and humanity to the frame. There should be lots to look at in a good shot of this kind, so use leading lines to take the viewer's eyes on a journey around the space.

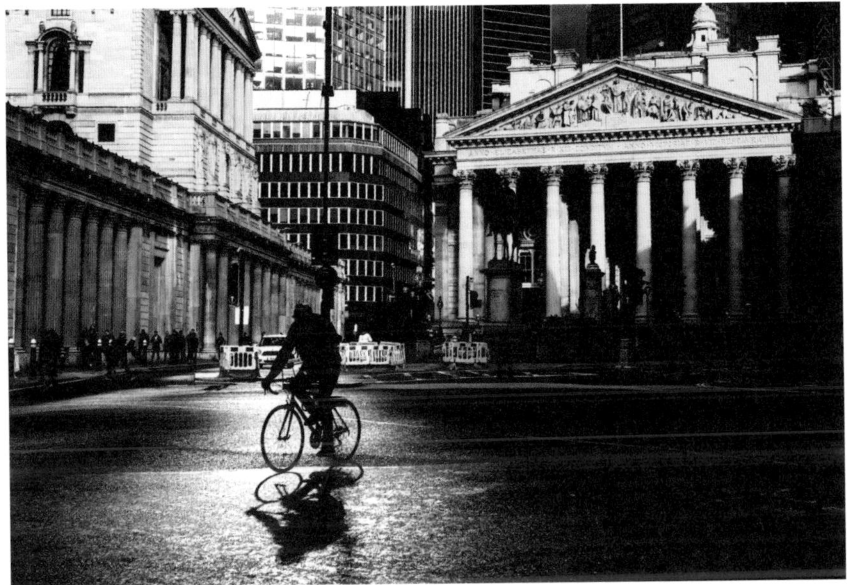

▲ *The cyclist sets up the scene, providing a human focal point for the expansive city backdrop.*

PRO TIPS

- Shooting urban landscapes isn't dependent on good weather. You can shoot great images in the rain, snow, or fog—or even on a gray day.
- Consider using a slow shutter speed (1/8 sec. or slower) to get some motion blur from people or traffic. You could even try it at night to get some great light trails.

TECHNIQUE

- Possibilities for abstracts are all around us. You simply need to train your eye to spot the potential.
- Aim for visual harmony in your image: experiment with composition to create balance and proportion.
- Try to work with simple objects that have clear, well-defined shapes.
- Explore your subject from different angles to see how it changes according to perspective and light.

IN THE ABSTRACT

Your mission here is to let your imagination run wild and create a monochrome abstract. One definition of an abstract is "a visual image that does not have an immediate association with the object world." Color often plays a big part in abstraction, so when there is an absence of color we need to make the other elements (form, texture, pattern, shape, and tonal range) work harder.

When looking for material to shoot for your abstract image, you'll need to view the world in a different way. Spend time looking at even the most mundane things for creative inspiration, anything from a disused phone box to a pile of bricks. The challenge is to transform your subject from the ordinary to the extraordinary. Look for a subject that you would regularly encounter in your daily life and try to visualize its abstract potential.

Remember, there are few rules and everything is possible. You're only constrained by your own imagination!

▲ *Try some intentional camera movement (ICM) with a slow shutter speed to turn a conventional shot into an abstract one.*

PRO TIPS

- Experiment with a macro lens. It can be fascinating to use the concept of proximity to make abstracts out of everyday objects.
- Create mystery or intrigue by making the viewer work a little harder to identify what the subject is.
- With an abstract, you're "allowed" to go beyond normal boundaries with editing. Use post-processing software to accentuate or emphasize certain features in your frame.

ASSIGNMENT JOURNAL

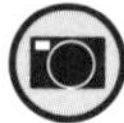

TECHNIQUE

- Look for contrasts. Define your area of negative space using tone or form.
- Approach this with real intent: know what you want to say and let the negative space help you say it.

EMBRACE THE SPACE

Negative space refers to the "unused" space around the main subject in your frame and helps to create a relationship between the focal point and the background. It's a technique that artists and designers often use to emphasize what's important in a picture, allowing the main subject (the positive space) to really stand out and grab the viewer's attention.

The space around your subject can be just as important as the subject itself and should be considered on equal terms. Sometimes, negative space is just "there," and other times, you can purposefully use it to your advantage.

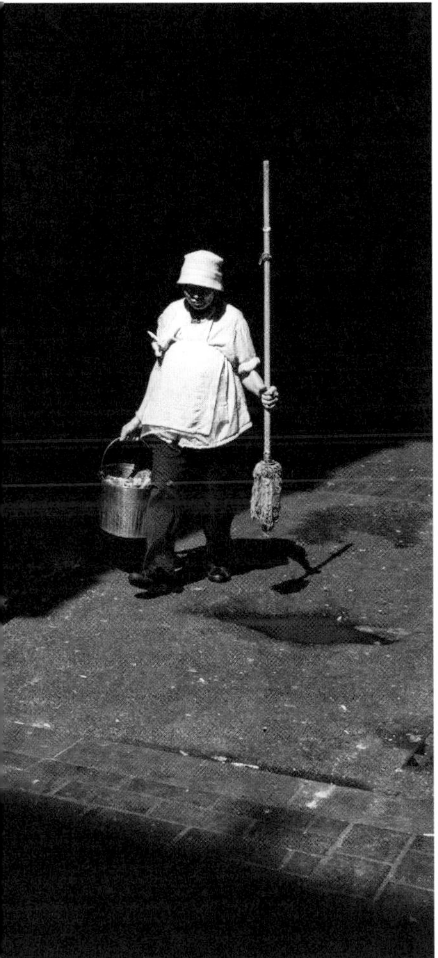

Your assignment is to find a scene and work out how to use negative space to help tell a story, perhaps by conveying feelings of isolation or contemplation, or creating a sense of intrigue or mystery.

◀ *The woman's white clothing really pops against the black negative space, which, combined with her awkward positioning towards the edge of the frame, helps create a feeling of insignificance or displacement.*

PRO TIPS

- Don't get too hung up on following compositional rules. Instead, use the combination of negative space and the unusual positioning of your subject (or subjects) for dramatic effect.
- Using a wider lens can help enhance the feeling of space, as can shooting from a low viewpoint.

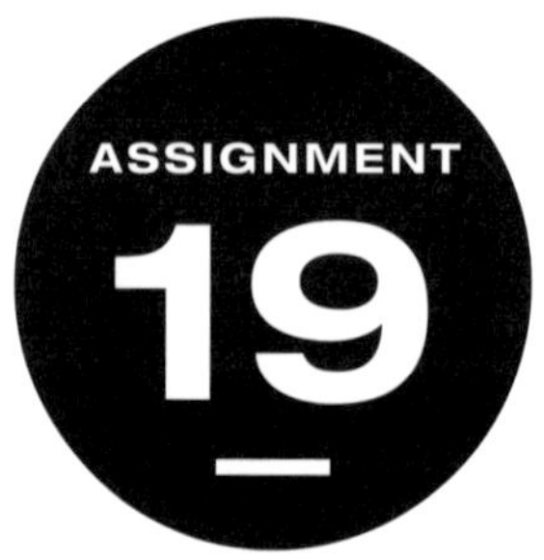

TECHNIQUE

- Try to replicate the same "film" characteristics in all your shots (use a similar ISO and shoot scenes with similar levels of contrast).
- Your mini project should have a consistent and cohesive theme, rather than being a collection of unconnected images. Your theme could be based on a narrative or perhaps a common aesthetic quality.

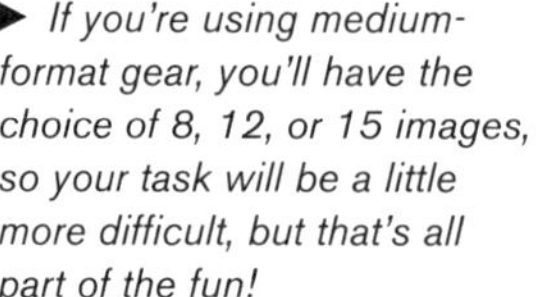

► *If you're using medium-format gear, you'll have the choice of 8, 12, or 15 images, so your task will be a little more difficult, but that's all part of the fun!*

ON A ROLL

This is the "one-roll challenge." Your brief is to take one roll of black-and-white film, giving you 36 exposures if you're using 35mm (or fewer if you're using medium format), and complete a project in one week using that one film. If you don't have a film camera, use the same discipline with your digital camera—and don't cheat! Some photographers work well under pressure, and a tight deadline like this can really make those creative juices flow.

This assignment is a great exercise in "slow photography," designed to make you think that little bit harder before pressing the shutter. Organize yourself early and plan well in advance so you can spend your seven days occupied purely with shooting. If you need ideas for your project, a good starting point is to look through your archive to see if it offers any inspiration.

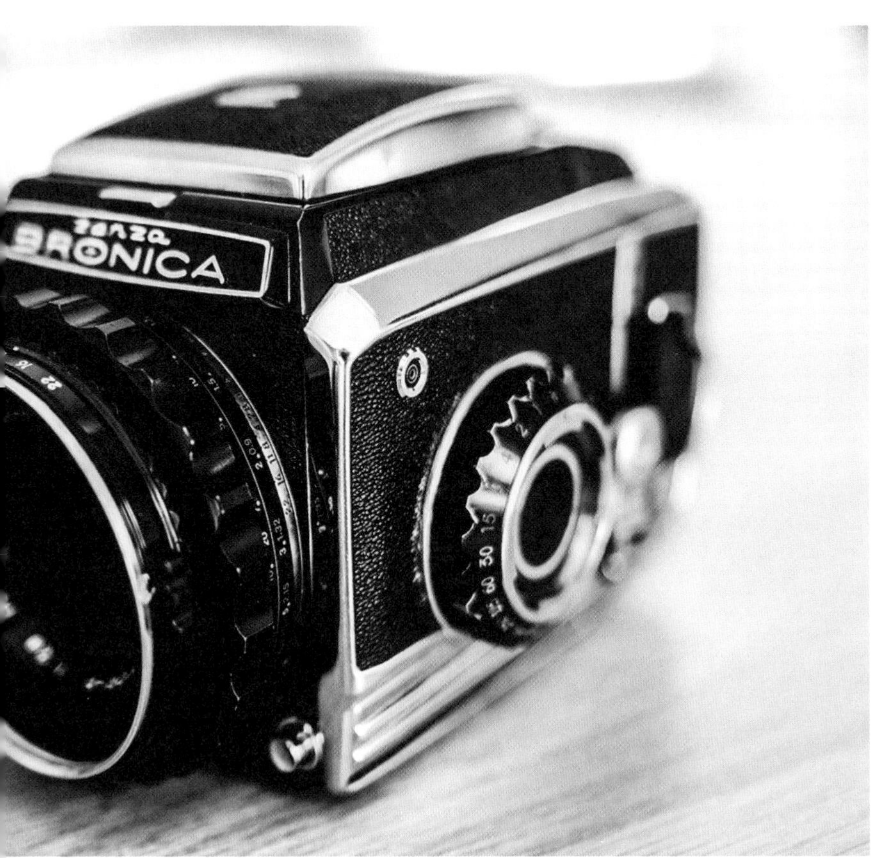

PRO TIPS

- This is a great learning exercise, so make sure you stick to the rules. Use your allotted number of images and no more.
- Work out a plan in advance. You'll probably struggle if you leave it to chance.
- Consider sharing your project once it's complete. You could produce a set of postcards or framed prints. Alternatively, you could write a blog post or share the project on your social media platforms.
- Use a slow, deliberate approach, taking care to avoid the obvious gaffes, such as camera shake or wildly incorrect exposure.

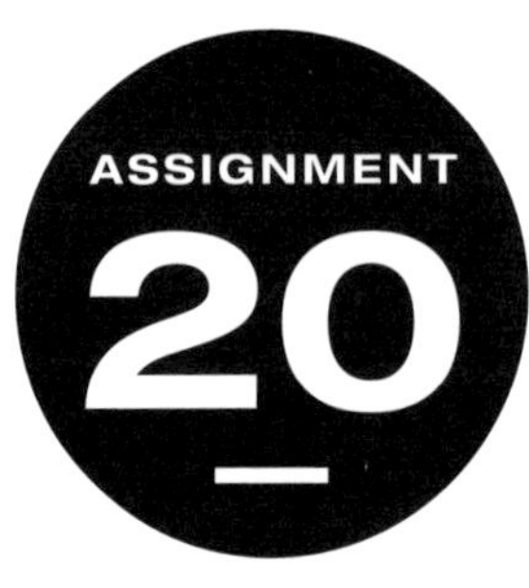

TECHNIQUE

- Move forward or backward as you view the scene. You'll see how the relationship between the layers changes and eventually find your perfect composition.
- Use tonality to make distinctions between the layers.
- A wideangle lens (24 or 28mm) will help you to incorporate an all-important foreground layer.
- The ideal starting point is to have three layers. You can have as many layers as you like in your image, but bear in mind that complex images are often more difficult for the viewer to understand.

LAYER CAKE

Photography is a two-dimensional art form and images can often look quite "flat." However, you can create an illusion of depth by using layers, or "planes," and this is a technique that works particularly well when shooting in black and white.

For this assignment, you will be experimenting with the concept of layers by examining different scenes through a series of planes within the frame, from front to back. Each plane should contain something that catches the eye and causes it to move through the frame and onto the next plane. An easy way to think of these planes is in terms of the foreground, middle ground, and background.

Aim to have something of interest on each of these layers and your images will immediately have more "volume."

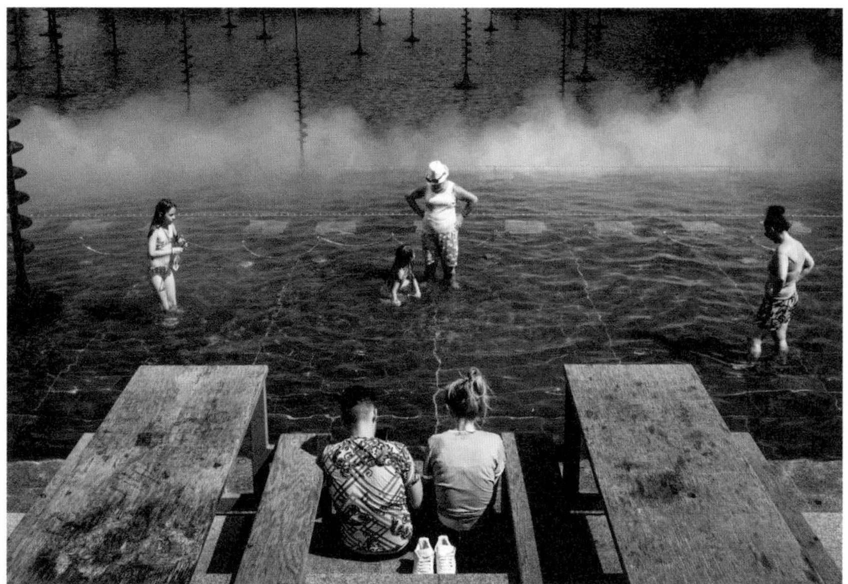

▲ *There's a logical journey for the eye to take, from the front of the frame toward the back.*

PRO TIPS

- It doesn't matter if one of your layers is soft, as this can add to the illusion of depth.
- Get into the habit of seeing the world around you as a series of layers. It's a great way to practice your compositional skills.
- Although this isn't an absolute rule, by placing your main subject on the middle layer you'll achieve a nice sense of balance.

ASSIGNMENT JOURNAL

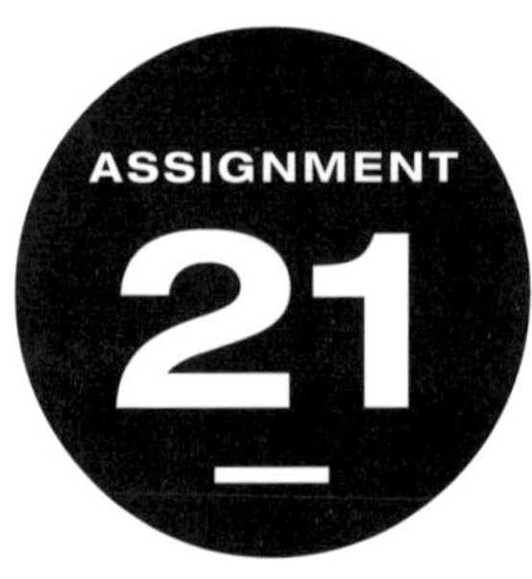

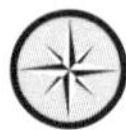

TECHNIQUE

- Be prepared to shoot at a high ISO. Markets often have very mixed sources of light, so shooting in monochrome should be a breeze. If the light is too low, don't worry—a bit of grain can add to the atmosphere (and markets are often all about atmosphere).
- Sometimes you'll want everything in focus, other times you'll want a shallow depth of field, so shoot in Aperture Priority mode and choose the aperture to suit the scene.
- A standard zoom lens (around 24–70mm) is ideal.
- Try to avoid using flash as it can kill any atmosphere. Seek out areas of natural light, instead.

TRADE SECRETS

In this assignment, you'll be heading to your local market and looking to turn the character and colors of the scene into a set of monochrome images.

The idea here is to go beyond the obvious and avoid taking shots usually associated with markets–the transaction between trader and customer, for example. Instead, look at what's going on around the fringes, away from the main arena; look below and above you; and check out the deliveries happening at the back of the stalls. Also, keep an eye out for the unusual in the usual—those offbeat moments that can bring a wry smile to your face.

You may find that you get a few stunning prints out of this assignment. If you're shooting in a local market, try asking the surrounding coffee shops and bars if they would like to display your prints—you might even sell some!

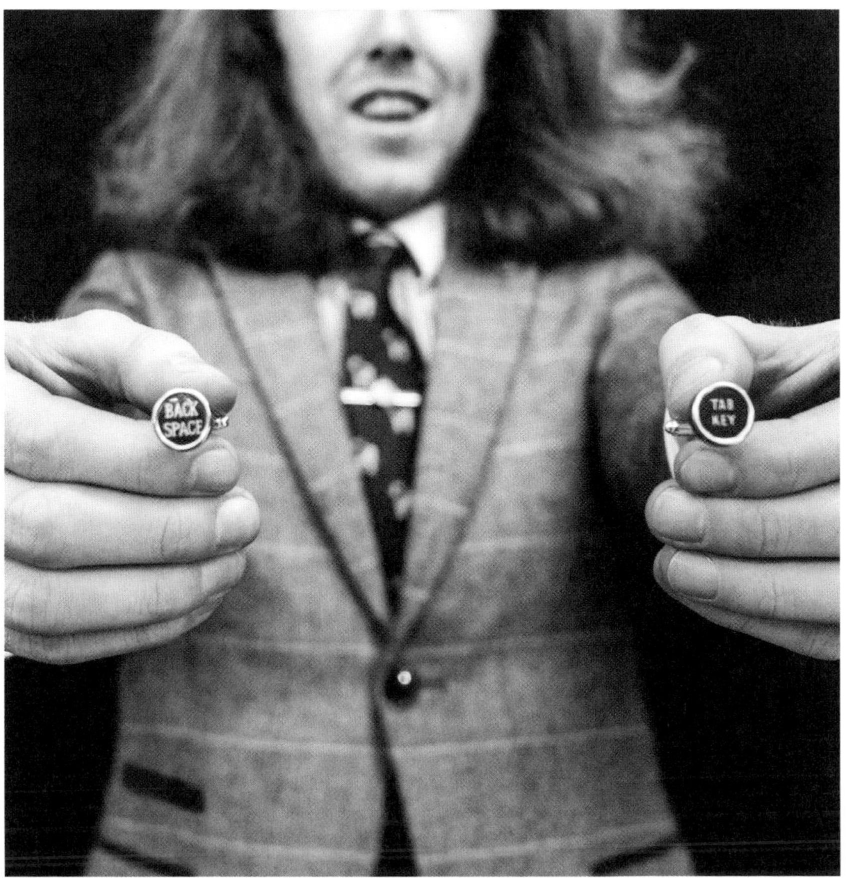

▲ *You'll find plenty of interesting characters in street markets and many will be happy to pose for you. You can choose to either ask first or just snap away, but be prepared to be barked at!*

PRO TIPS

- Look out for steam or smoke—often found in markets selling cooked food—as these can add an atmospheric quality.
- It's nice to buy something to help the traders, but don't pay for photos.
- Vary your viewpoint: try shooting from low and high positions.
- If you're traveling overseas, learn about (and be sensitive to) the local culture, so that you're not upsetting people and you feel more "accepted."

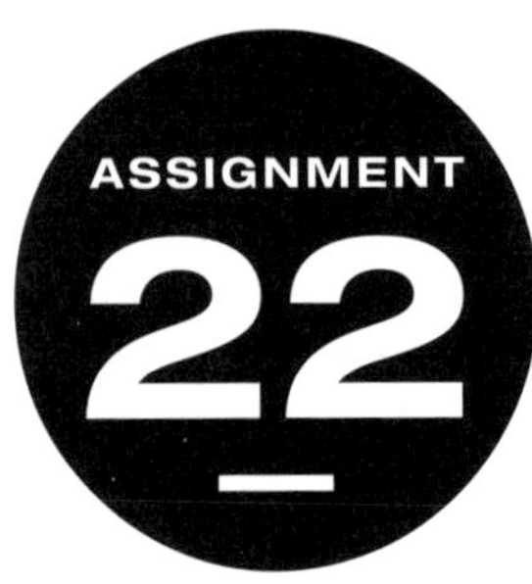

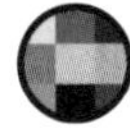

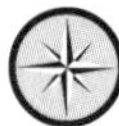

TECHNIQUE

- Choose a viewpoint close to the buildings and shoot wide. You should always be looking up at your subject.
- You'll want plenty of depth of field, so choose a small aperture (f/11 or f/16 is ideal).
- To help maximize depth of field, focus on a point roughly a third of the way into the frame.
- Capture your image on a clear, bright day, ideally with a deep blue sky and fluffy white clouds, and use a red filter to darken the sky and make the clouds really stand out.
- The lower the viewpoint, the greater the effect, so get down to ground level for added drama.
- Find a composition that includes the corners or edges of buildings. This will make them look more imposing.

PRO TIPS

- Use a wideangle lens to create the most dramatic effect; a lens between 16 and 28mm usually works well.
- Decide whether you want to include reflections or not. If you don't, use a polarizer.

ASSIGNMENT JOURNAL

TOWERING ABOVE

One of the issues we come up against when photographing tall buildings is converging verticals. We can counter this effect by using an expensive tilt-shift lens or by straightening up these lines in post-processing. Alternatively, we can embrace the effect and use it to our advantage, which is what you're going to do in this assignment.

If you're shooting tall structures, converging verticals is always going to occur, so, rather than worrying about it, let's use the effect to create a "wow" factor. Choose a bright day and find yourself a tall, angular building with crisp lines and, ideally, plenty of reflective surfaces. Let the verticals converge, then capture your stunning black-and-white image.

▼ *Don't be afraid of high contrast. The inclusion of some white clouds can add a little extra contrast to your frame.*

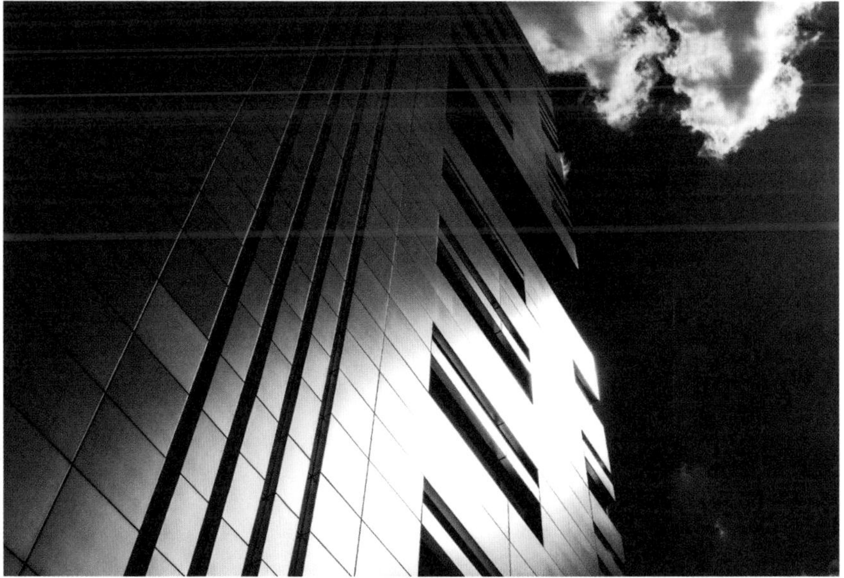

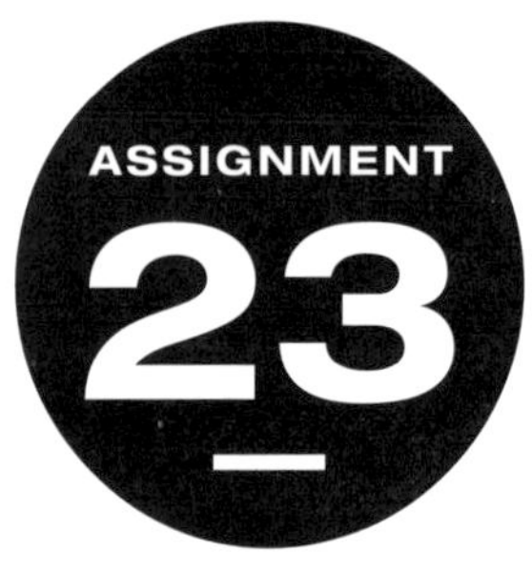

TECHNIQUE

- A good starting point is to look for strong lines. Diagonal lines add tension and can draw the viewer's eye to a particular part of the frame.
- Try different viewpoints. The direction of the light can have a significant impact on the graphical character of your shot.
- Bear in mind that shape can determine mood. Hard lines, such as triangles, are more aggressive, whereas circles or curves convey a softer feel.
- Play with the Color Mixer sliders in your post-processing software to emphasize or enhance certain areas within the frame. This can be an effective way of manipulating the contrast in a black-and-white image.

WORK THE ANGLES

Strong lines and angles can really help to inspire and create striking images. They can be found everywhere—from the interiors of your own home and workplace to the local gallery—so the key to this assignment is spotting the potential (the graphical qualities) of things that surround us in everyday life.

Inspiration can be found in architecture, shadows, road markings, signs, and the natural world, as well as the small details of cars, buildings, and machinery. Approach this project with an open mind, as things that at any other time might seem uninspiring may just surprise you.

You should aim to find subject matter that complements the black-and-white medium: look for high-contrast compositions with strong angular lines, swooping curves, or bold shapes.

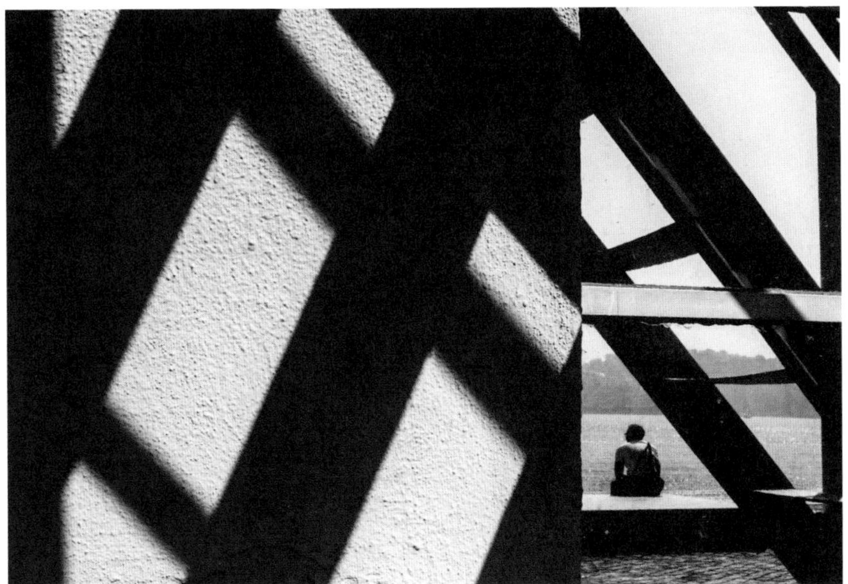

▲ *Shadows can form strong graphical patterns and, on a sunny day, there's potential for them everywhere.*

PRO TIPS

- If you can, set your viewfinder to monochrome to give a clear view of shape and form and to judge the effects of the light.
- If you're short of ideas, look at modern architecture, where you'll usually find striking graphical influences.
- Don't overlook "boring" objects. If you get the angle and lighting right, many seemingly mundane things have unexpected graphical potential.

ASSIGNMENT JOURNAL

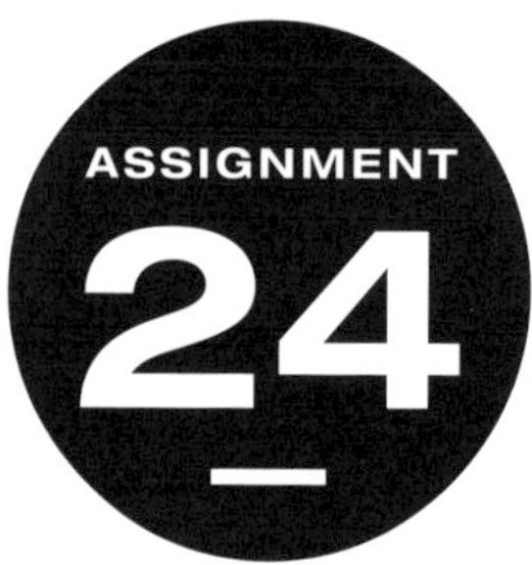

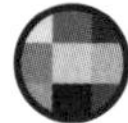

TECHNIQUE

- Choose a bold, well-defined subject. If there's more than one person in the shot, make sure there's space between them so that they don't appear as a big black blob.
- Strong backlighting is essential. It needn't be direct light, just strong enough to overpower the subject.
- Expose for the background. If you let the camera do the work by using Aperture Priority, it will usually expose the scene perfectly. If you need the subject to be a little darker, try dialing in a stop or two of underexposure using exposure compensation.

▼ *The shape is really important in a silhouette shot. The crisp outline of this subject and his bag makes for an elegant shot.*

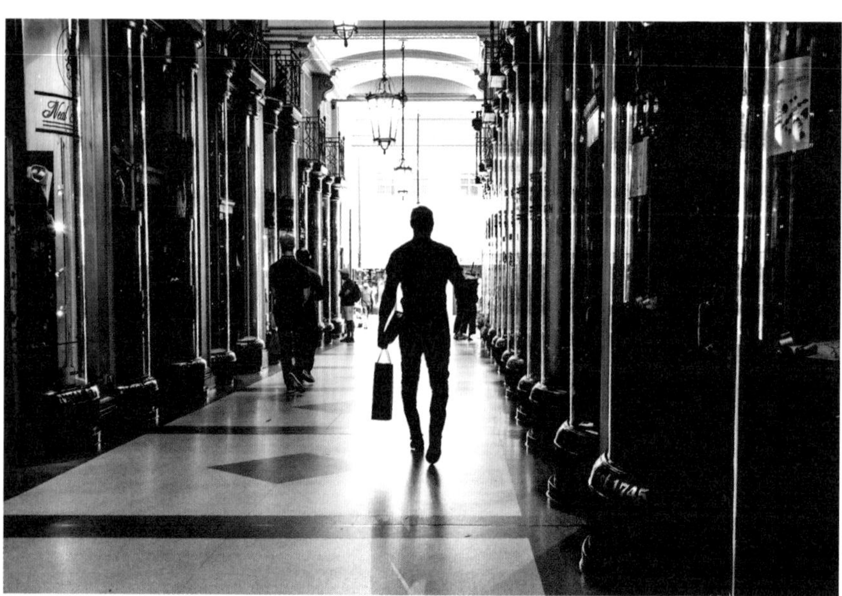

DRAMATIC OUTLINES

It's hard to argue with the simple elegance of a good silhouette. A strong shape, good backlighting, and a crisp composition can all add up to a stylish monochrome image and, in this assignment, your task is to add drama to that list.

The key consideration here should always be the light. Strong light equals strong contrast, and that's exactly what is a required for a silhouette. Your subject could be anything, although this will work particularly well with people, where the absence of detail can help create a sense of mystery.

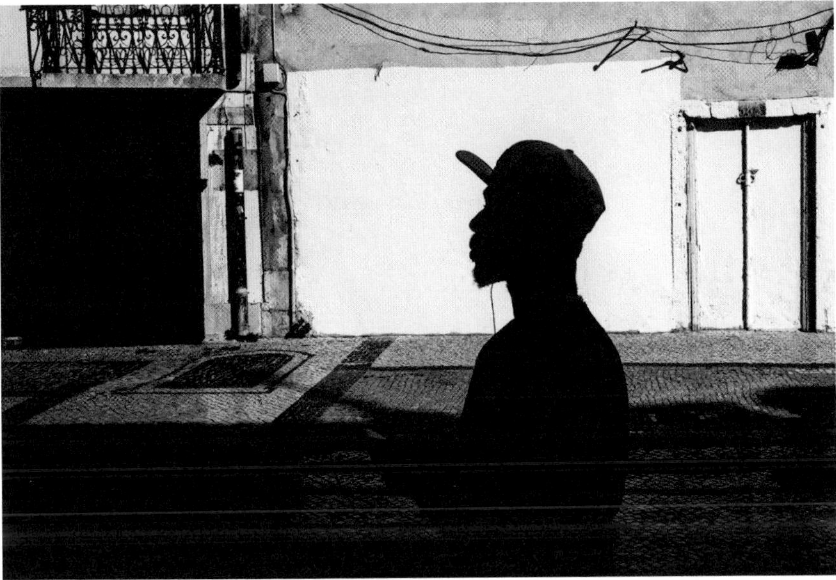

▲ *Placing the head in the white frame helps to emphasize the silhouette in this picture, taken in Lisbon, Portugal.*

PRO TIPS

- As there won't be much light on the subject, your auto focus may struggle, so try focusing manually instead.
- If your background is the sky, experiment with shooting from a lower position to eliminate unwanted distractions.
- If you find that you're struggling to judge the light accurately, bracketing may help you achieve the correct exposure.

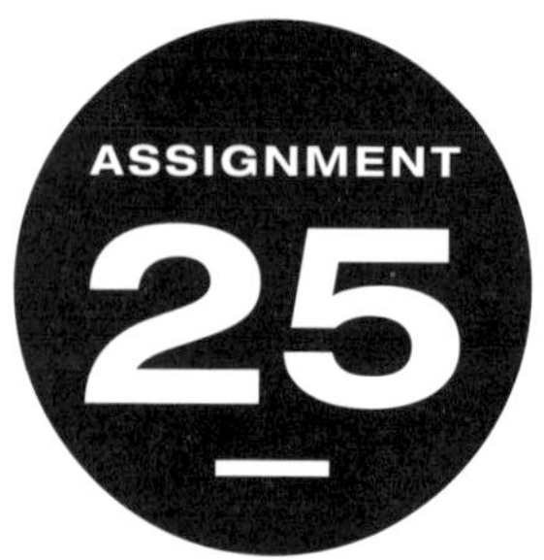

TECHNIQUE

- Don't worry too much about grain (noise), as it can add to the retro vibe.
- Use composition, rather than post-processing tools, to remove or exclude "modern" elements from your frame.
- Be careful of contradictions. For example, old photos are often less "contrasty," so keep this in mind when using 21st-century post-processing techniques on your images.

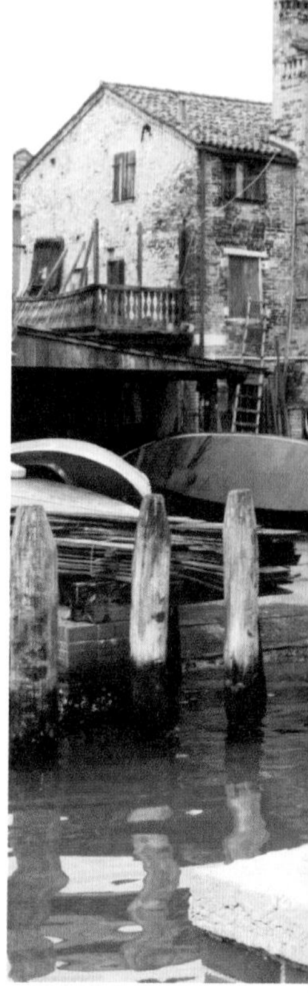

TIME STANDS STILL

Pictures are sometimes described as having a "timeless" quality. Although these images tend to be difficult to date exactly, which is part of their appeal, they usually evoke the feeling of a time gone by.

In this assignment, your mission is to capture an enduring image—something that audiences will be able to relate to in years to come—that has a vintage feel. This isn't about dressing your relatives in Victorian costumes and shooting them with a sepia filter; it's about shooting life as it is today, but trying to avoid any references to 21st-century living.

Unfortunately, it's not as easy as you might think. Everywhere you look there is evidence of modern life and you'll have to work hard to exclude it. This exercise will be a great test of your observational and compositional skills. Think about it as being composition in reverse. In other words, excluding elements in the frame, rather than including them.

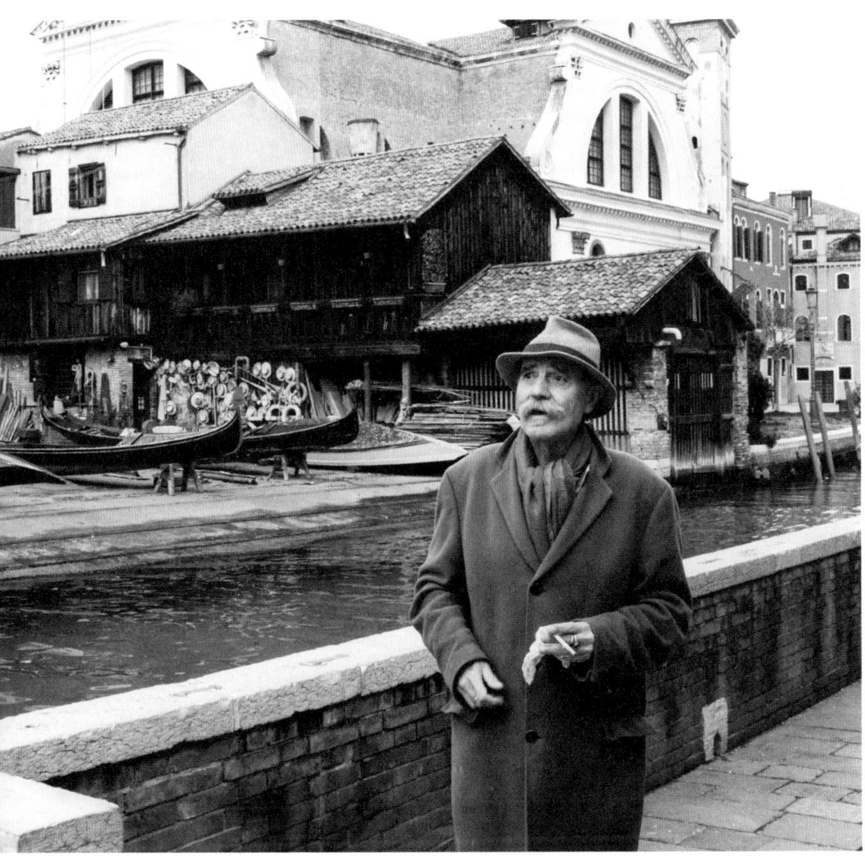

▲ *With virtually no references to modern life, this could have been shot 50 years ago.*

PRO TIPS

- Give yourself a head start by choosing subjects with a "timeless" quality, such as those wearing traditional coats and hats.
- Attend events, such as vintage fairs, revivals, and classic car shows, where there will be lots of photogenic subject matter and people are generally very happy to have their picture taken.
- Once you get into the spirit of this you'll probably find that it's both fun and challenging. It may even lead to a more long-term project.

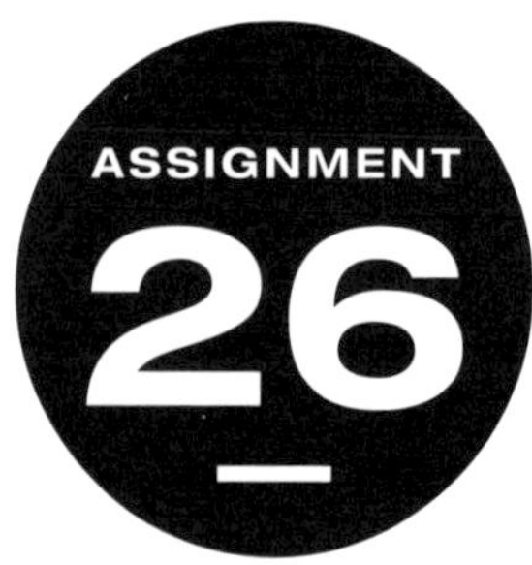

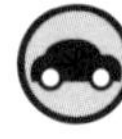

TECHNIQUE

- Look for really strong graphics. If the words are big and bold, your image will have more impact.
- Be prepared to wait. You may see the potential in a background, but you'll need a second element to make the connection. Street photographers call this "fishing" and it's a very popular pursuit!
- Signs often have more visual impact when shot square-on rather than at an angle.

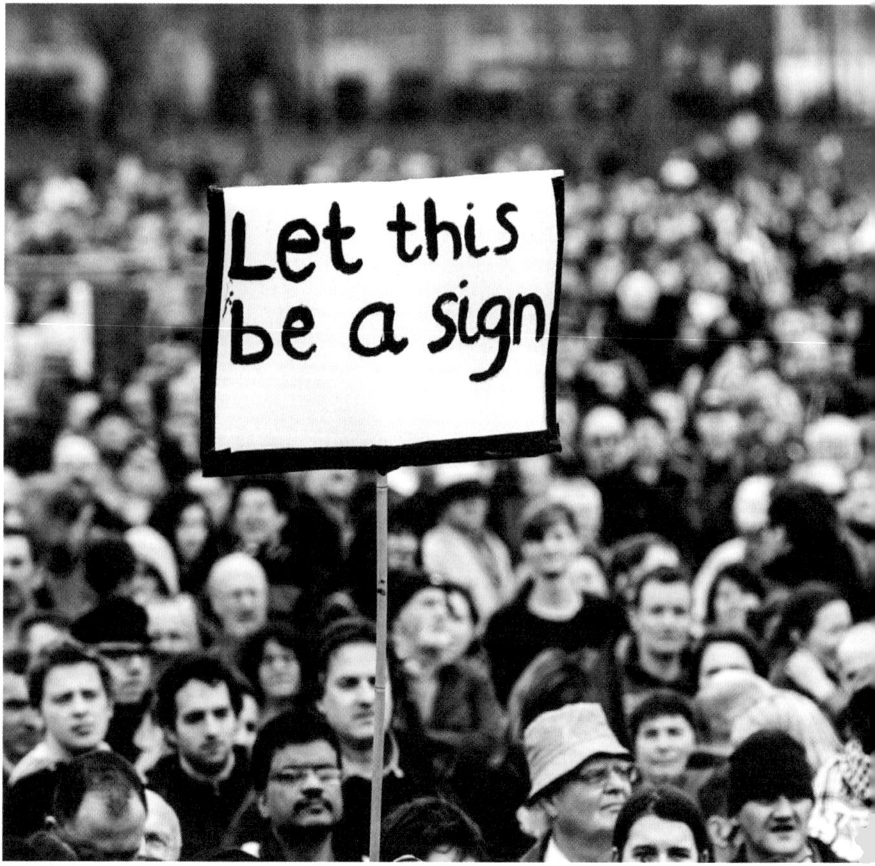

WORDPLAY

The written word has always had an important role to play in the world of street photography, and can be found in the form of advertisements, road signs, public information notices, brand logos, even car license plates.

For this assignment, your brief is to take a photograph that makes a humorous connection between the written word and something in close proximity to it. This form of juxtaposition is easy to do, but you do need to be very observant and take in the detail all around you.

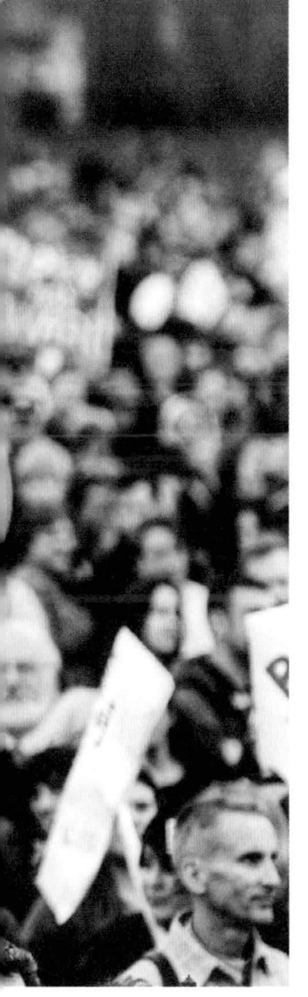

PRO TIPS

- When you're walking the streets (with or without your camera), make a conscious effort to take notice of all the words around you. This will sharpen your observation skills and open your mind to possible connections.
- Street photographers are sometimes accused of ridiculing people, and it's an easy trap to fall into. There's no need to offend anyone; shots like these are just as engaging with some warm and gentle wit.

ASSIGNMENT JOURNAL

◀ *Always consider how the words will work in monochrome and whether they will stand out sufficiently from the background.*

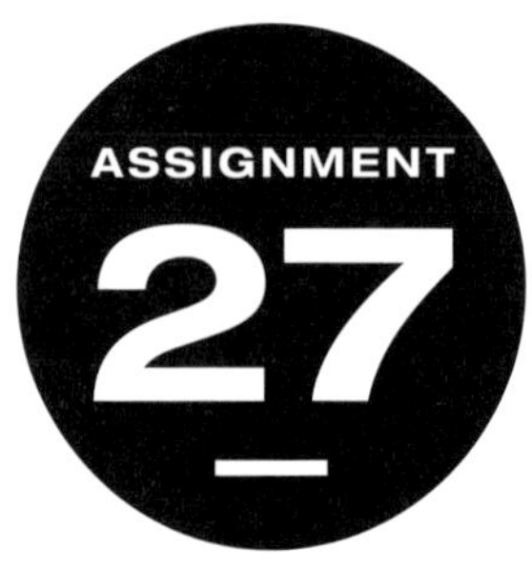

TECHNIQUE

- Experiment with shutter speeds. Use a fast speed (at least 1/500 sec.) to freeze the movement of water, or a slow one (1/4 sec. or slower) to create a smooth, blurred effect.
- To allow for a very slow shutter speed, you may need to use a neutral density (ND) filter to control the amount of light entering the camera.
- A dark background will make white water much more visible, so choose your shooting position carefully.
- If you want to minimize reflections, use a polarizing filter.
- When it's raining, give the Clarity slider a good nudge to the right in post-processing to make the falling rain stand out.

ASSIGNMENT JOURNAL

PRO TIPS

- If you're going for a blurred effect, the closer you are to the water, the more pronounced the effect will be.
- Shooting fast-moving water (a waterfall, for example) is best done on an overcast day, as this will minimize unwanted reflections.
- Look into puddles for some great reflection shots. Get down to the level of the puddle and use a wideangle lens with a small aperture for maximum depth of field.
- Take care with the highlights when shooting white water–use your histogram for guidance.

GO WITH THE FLOW

Water is all around us and, whether it's rainwater, the ocean, a lake, a canal, or something in a bottle, it's all quite photogenic. One of the benefits of shooting water in black and white is that you'll often get good contrast between the water and the background.

There are many ways of capturing water and an array of subjects to choose from. You could shoot crashing waves, heavy rain, or a bubbling stream, or you could create something more abstract. Whatever you decide to focus on, your challenge in this assignment is to photograph water creatively.

▼ *Waterfalls make great subjects for a slow shutter speed shot, and a polarizer will reduce the reflections.*

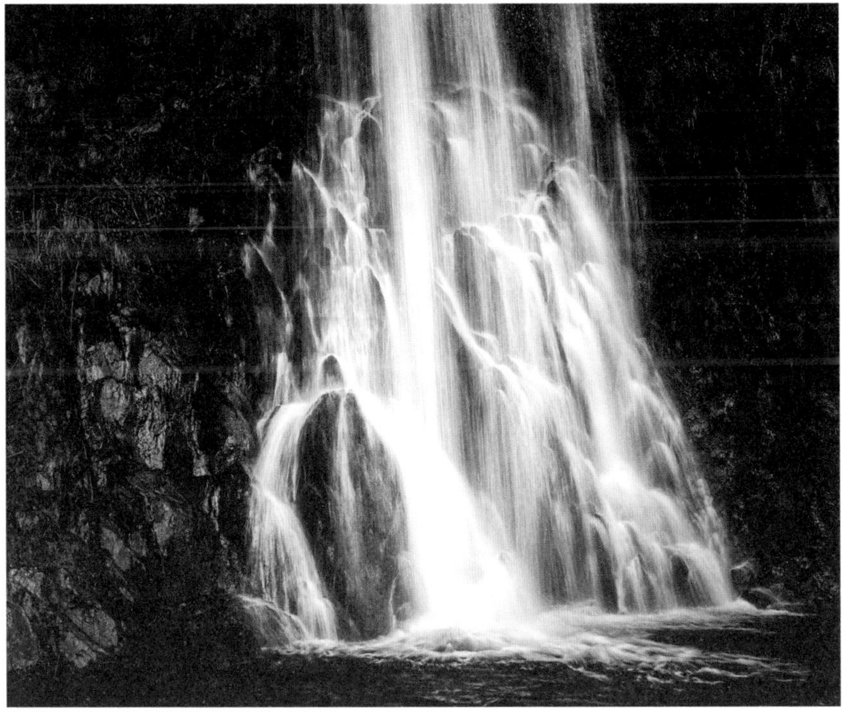

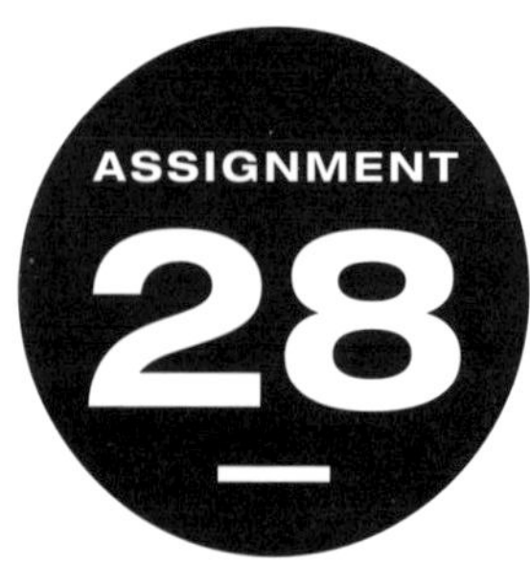

TECHNIQUE

- Aim for a consistent look and feel to the images–the more cohesive the style, the more professional the finished product will look.
- Try to get a "soft" proof from the printer. This small investment will give you peace of mind and prevent expensive mistakes.
- Once your zine is printed, make sure you spread the word—they're no good sitting in a box under your desk!

HOT OFF THE PRESS

Zines (short for "magazines") have never been more popular in the world of photography. They are small booklets, often 8.3 x 5.8in (210 x 148mm), and usually contain somewhere between 20 and 60 images. This is a brilliant and cost-effective way to present your work, and it's incredibly easy to do.

Your brief is to create your own zine. This is much easier to do than you might think. Follow these steps to make your zine production a straightforward process.

HOW TO CREATE A ZINE

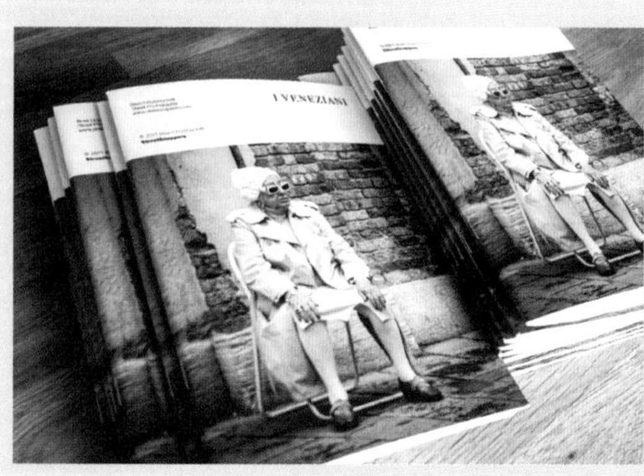

1 Choose your theme. Zines work best when they're based on a specific theme, rather than a random collection of images.

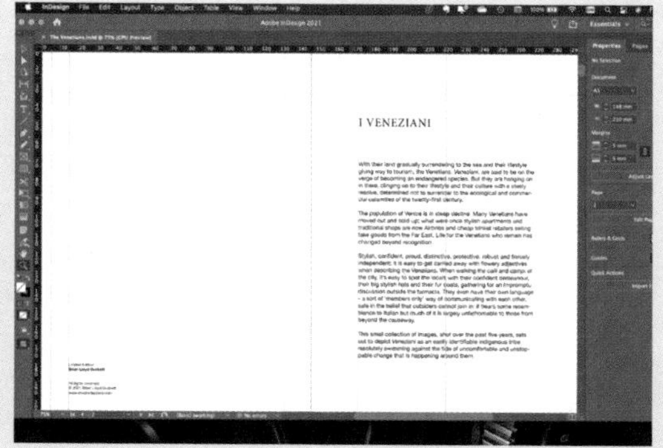

2 Decide on a page count by working out how many images you want to include, allowing for one image per page. The number of pages will go up in multiples of four (12, 16, 20, etc.). Don't forget to allow for front and back covers, and space for an introduction.

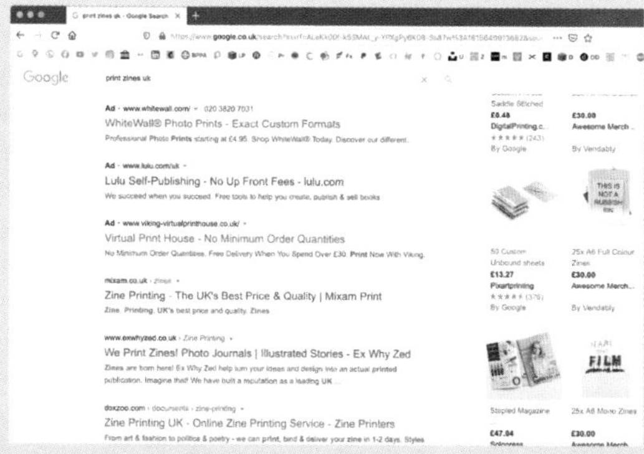

3 Choose a company to print your zine. If you don't know of any, a web search is a good place to start. They don't need to be local to you, as most will undertake the whole process online.

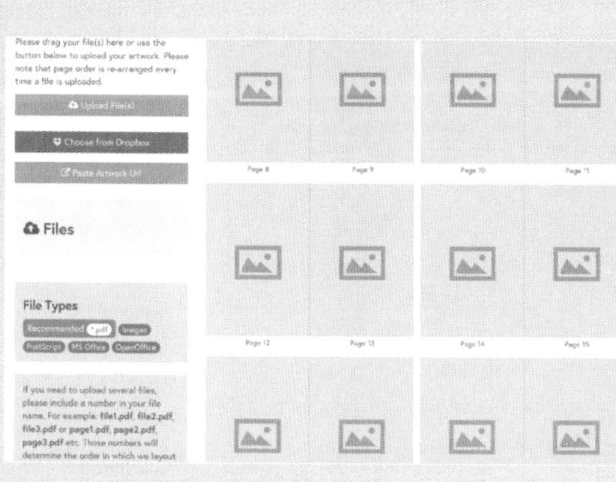

4 Prepare your images for print, following the printing company's guidelines for image sizing, color space, and so on.

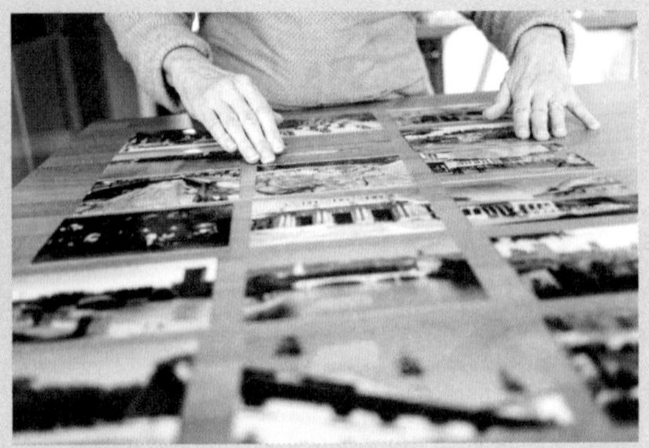

5 Think about the sequence of your images. Ensure there's a logical flow from beginning to end and that photos on facing pages work well together. Print a small version of each image, spread them all out on a table, and shuffle them around until you're happy.

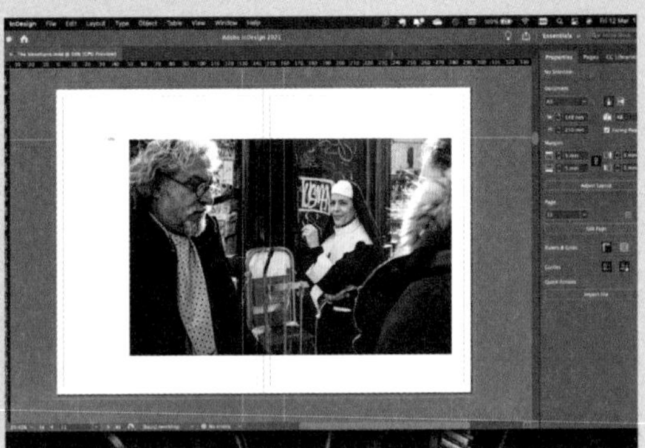

6 It's time to design your zine. If you're adept at Adobe InDesign, you can design it yourself and send the finished files to the printer. Alternatively, many printers have a "drag and drop" image-upload facility, which makes the whole process very easy.

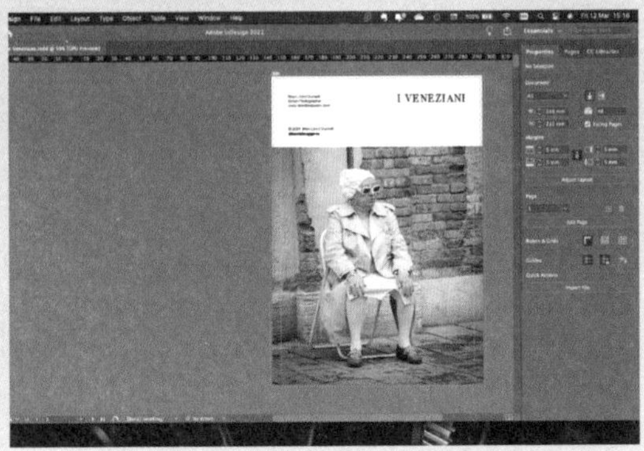

7 Once your images are uploaded, you'll need to make decisions about the finish and weight of the paper for the inside pages and the cover; the paper size; and the type of binding (stapling is usually cheapest).

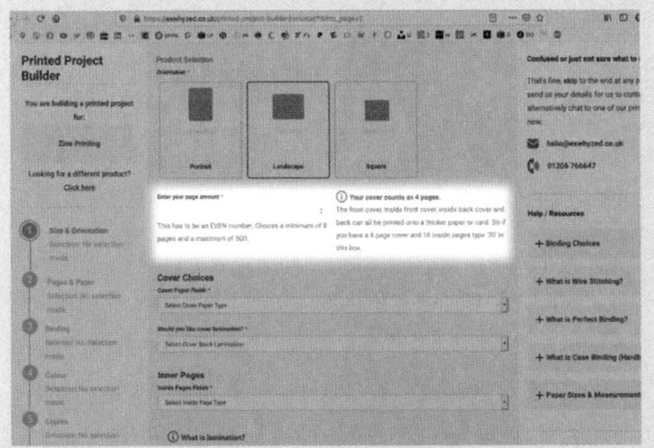

8 Decide on the quantity you're going to have printed. Some printers will produce as few as 25 copies, but a print run of 50 or 100 will be more economical.

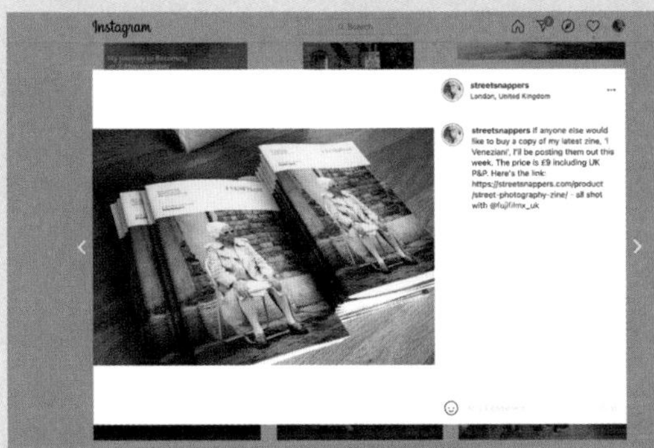

9 Finally, you need to consider what to do with your finished zine. Many people sell their zines on their website or social media platforms, or through a local bookstore, gallery, or camera store. Alternatively, you can create your zine for fun and give copies to friends and family.

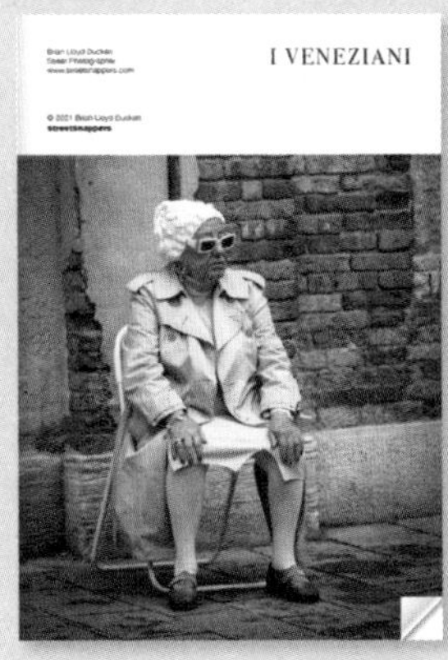

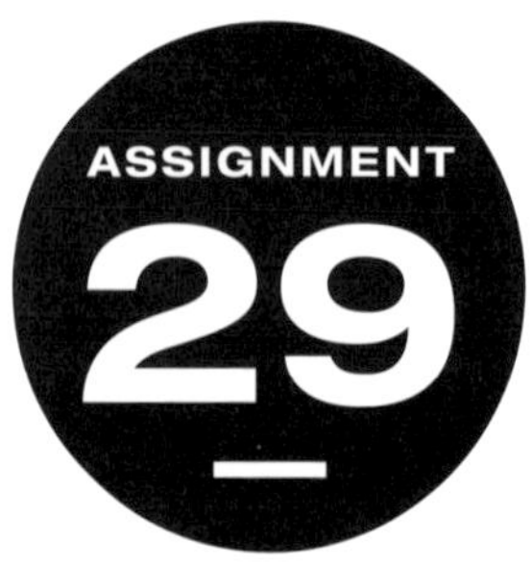

TECHNIQUE

- Get to know your subjects, then plan the shoot, aiming to tell mini stories through your images.
- Candid, informal images work better than formal, posed shots.
- You'll want to achieve bright images–a slightly overexposed look works well in lifestyle photography. Use natural light instead of flash.
- Shoot with a medium to wide aperture (f/5.6 or wider), ideally using a fast prime lens.

THE EVERYDAY

When we think of lifestyle photography we tend to think of vibrant colors, but it works equally well in black and white. In this assignment you're going to shoot a lifestyle session, which could be with family, friends, colleagues, clients, or even strangers.

True lifestyle photography is an artistic depiction of people doing what they normally do, so it shouldn't be overly staged. Your aim here is to capture "real" life, as it happens. Find your willing subjects and shoot them in a bright, everyday environment, anything from a kitchen to a cornfield. It doesn't really matter where the shoot takes place, as long as the surroundings feel authentic and natural.

Approach this project as a lifestyle photographer would an assignment: aim to capture around 24 images, which you could then present to your subjects as a photobook.

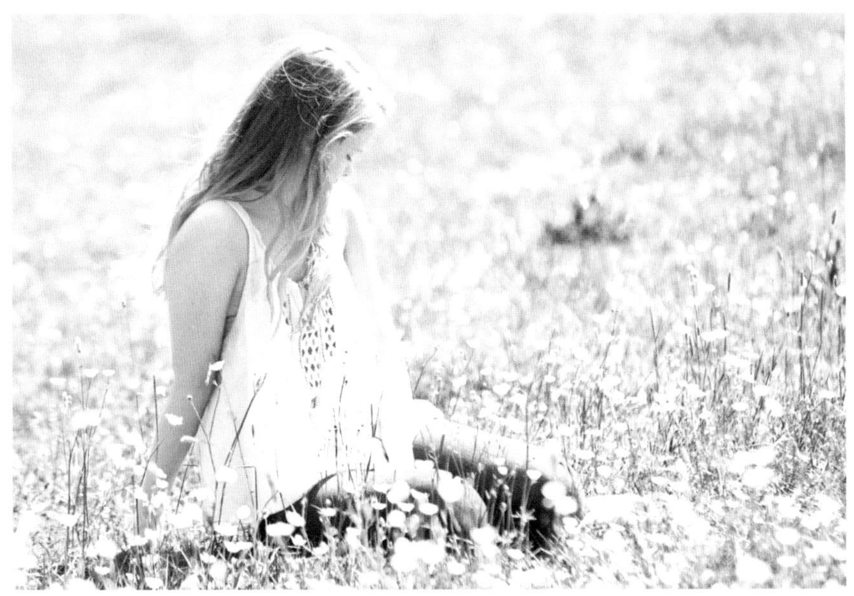

▲ *A bright, backlit environment is perfect for lifestyle photography. It's okay to overexpose slightly, as bright highlights will look great.*

PRO TIPS

- If you can, include a meaningful background or props in the shot to add context.
- Give your subjects something to do. This will make them relaxed and less aware of the camera.
- Aim for the perfect balance between directing and being a fly on the wall. This is a fine balance, so it will take practice to achieve.

ASSIGNMENT JOURNAL

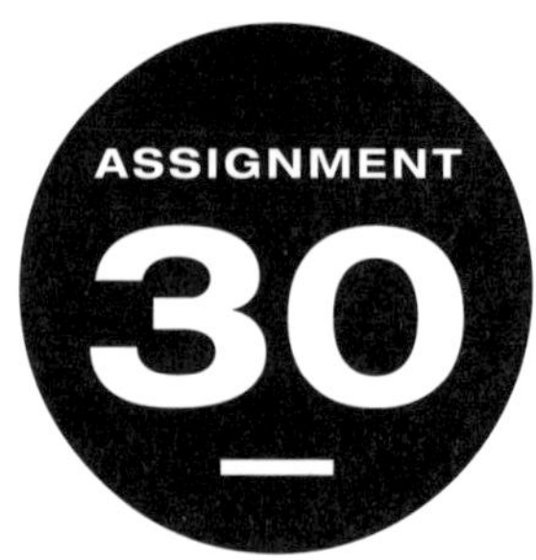

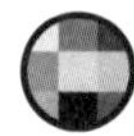
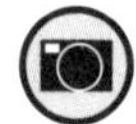

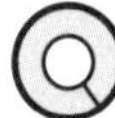

TECHNIQUE

- To achieve good contrast in the texture, avoid full-on, direct lighting. Instead, light your subject from the side.
- As you're shooting in black and white, tonality is crucial and it's best to avoid extreme levels of blacks or whites.
- Experiment with different angles. This will change how the light falls on your subject and can dramatically change its appearance.
- Unless you're going for a deliberate bokeh effect (see Assignment 42), you'll usually want sharpness across the frame, so use an aperture of f/5.6 or smaller. This may necessitate a slow shutter speed, so have your tripod handy.
- You can enhance texture in post-processing by using any combination of the Contrast, Texture, and Clarity sliders, but be careful not to overdo it.

SURFACE APPEAL

Texture is everywhere; wherever there's a surface, there's some sort of texture. And, happily for us, black and white is the perfect medium for these shots.

Finding a texture that inspires you shouldn't be difficult, as there are so many to choose from. Tree bark, rust, food, leaves, concrete, brickwork, fabric, peeling paint, human skin, and animal fur are just a few ideas. You have the option to shoot close-up (or even macro) or to take a much wider view.

When you're shooting a texture, the most important considerations are pattern, lighting, and depth. For this assignment, you should aim to produce an image that incorporates all three elements successfully.

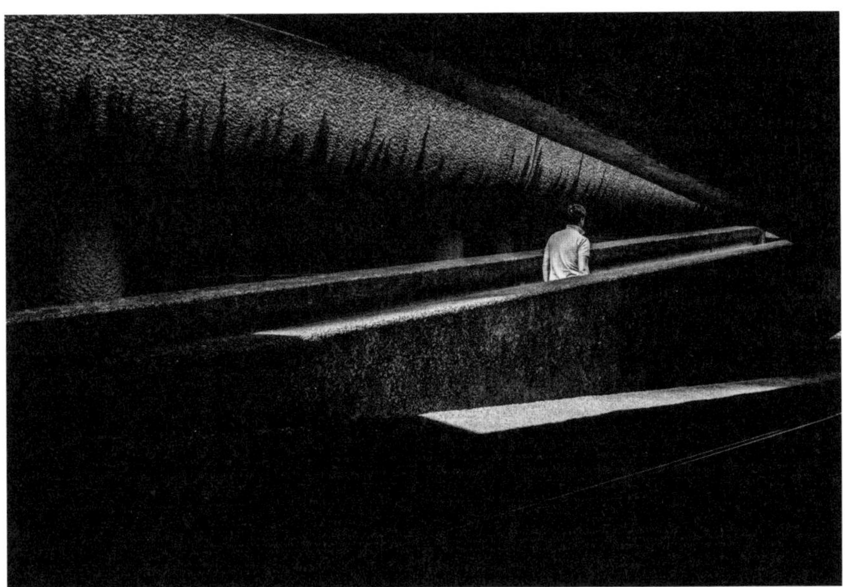

▲ *Modern buildings, particularly those built in the 1960s and '70s, often have a variety of richly textured surfaces, which translate very well into black and white.*

PRO TIPS

- If your camera has the facility, set the viewfinder to black and white so you can judge the effects of the light.
- Keep your eyes open—you'll find great textures in the most unlikely places.
- The way textures look will differ throughout the day as the light conditions change. Soft lighting created by a low sun often works well.
- Consider taking an abstract approach, as this is well suited to textures.

ASSIGNMENT JOURNAL

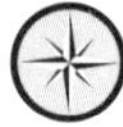

TECHNIQUE

- Plan your shoot. Find the best vantage point, then think about the position of the light at different times of the day.
- The quality, color, and angle of the light can make or break any shot, and this is especially true for urban landscape photography. A subject that looks dull and uninspiring at one time of the day can be transformed into a truly spellbinding image with the passing of just a few hours.
- Consider using a slow shutter speed to add a sense of movement to the scene.

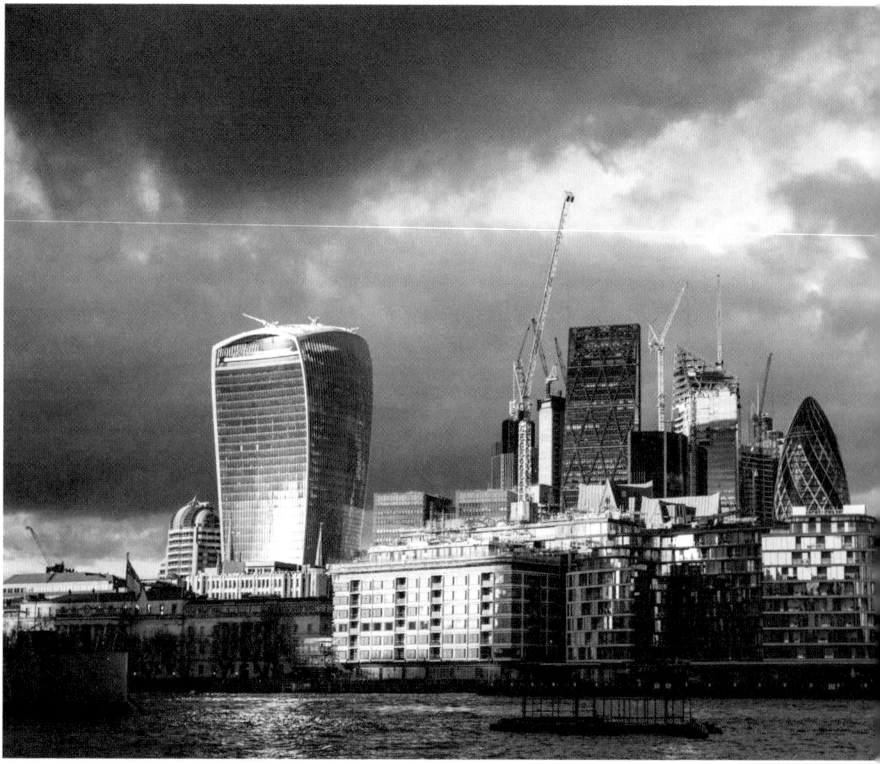

ESCAPE THE TOURIST TRAP

We have all taken the predictable "tourist" shots from a popular viewpoint and many of these images will look very similar. However, when we're shooting these scenes in monochrome, we can bring much more gravitas to these photographs and create something that may even warrant the "fine art" label.

Your task is to choose a popular location (you don't need to travel to an exotic location for this, just find a tourist spot near you) and shoot the scene in monochrome. Your image could be of a landscape or cityscape, or it could show a monument or iconic building.

Consider how you can use light and composition to further differentiate your image from other photographs of that same location. You could even experiment with abstract techniques, such as intentional camera movement (ICM) or motion blur.

ASSIGNMENT JOURNAL

◀ *The angry sky and the dramatic late-afternoon light help to distinguish this from the many thousands of shots of this viewpoint in London, UK.*

PRO TIPS

- You could turn this into a long-term project by shooting all the tourist locations you visit in this way, perhaps even continuing the assignment over a number of years.

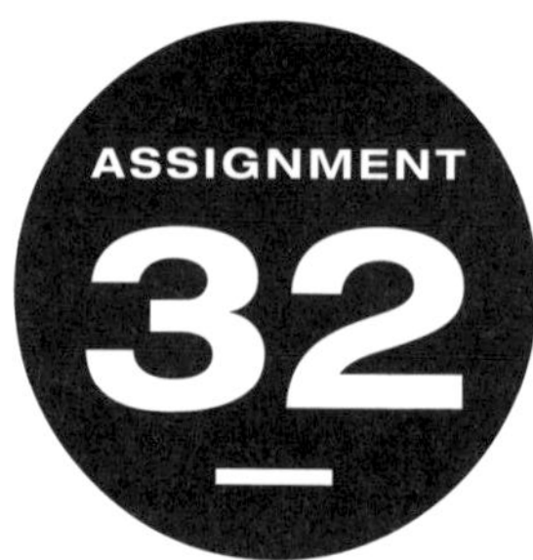

TECHNIQUE

- Be aware that a square image has no "sense of direction." The eye is drawn inward, toward the center of the frame, so placing your subject in the middle can work really well.
- Due to the above, the square format is better suited to stationary rather than dynamic subjects.
- Try symmetrical compositions. These are particularly suited to square frames.

▼ *The best way to really get into square shooting is to buy an old 120 film camera.*

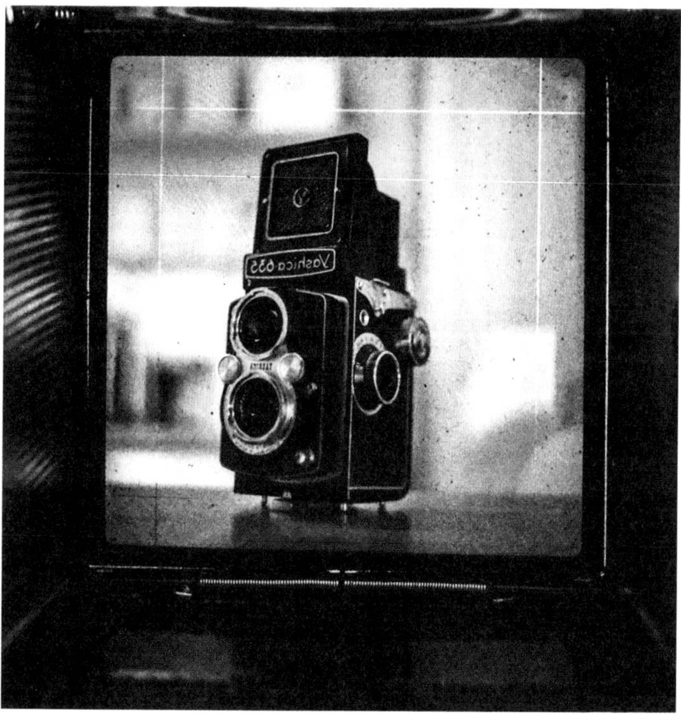

SQUARE UP

In the 1960s and '70s, the 2.4 x 2.4in (6 x 6cm) square negative dominated medium-format photography, with the likes of Hasselblad, Rolleiflex, and Bronica cameras being the weapon of choice for many professionals. The square format has enjoyed a resurgence in recent years, mainly thanks to Instagram, and many artists consider the square image to be a more intellectual composition compared to the plain old rectangle.

However, as we're so used to photographing in rectangles, composing to a square can be a bit of a challenge and that's what you'll be focusing on in this assignment. If you have a square-format camera then that's great, but you don't necessarily need one for this project (see overleaf).

Composing to a square format is a really useful training exercise and an effective way to get you thinking about composition. Try doing this consistently for a week or a month, preferably using the first method described on the next page.

▼ *Placing the key subject matter in the center of the frame works really well with a square.*

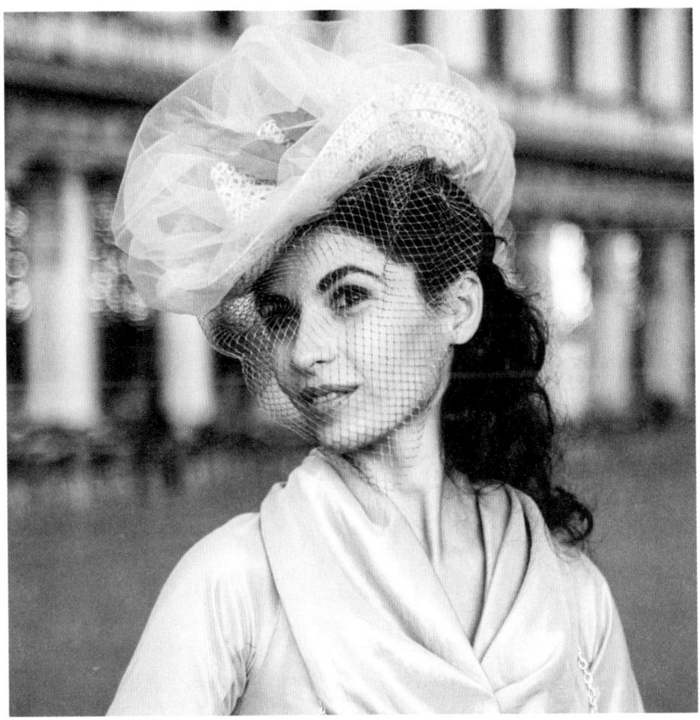

HOW TO COMPOSE TO A SQUARE FORMAT

There are three ways you can compose to a square format:

1 Visualize a square frame in your viewfinder and make your composition fit into it (this is a great way to learn and the recommended approach for this assignment).

2 Set your camera's aspect ratio to 1:1 (if available) to pre-set the image to a square format.

3 Crop your image to a square format in post-processing.

PRO TIPS

- Consider buying an old 120 format camera and start to have fun with film.
- To become familiar with the format, look over some of your old images and experiment with a square crop. This will help you "see" in squares.
- Simple, uncluttered compositions work particularly well as a square black-and-white image.
- Some digital cameras have a setting that allows you to change the picture size and shoot a square image.

▶ Don't forget to use other compositional techniques, such as leading lines, in your square compositions.

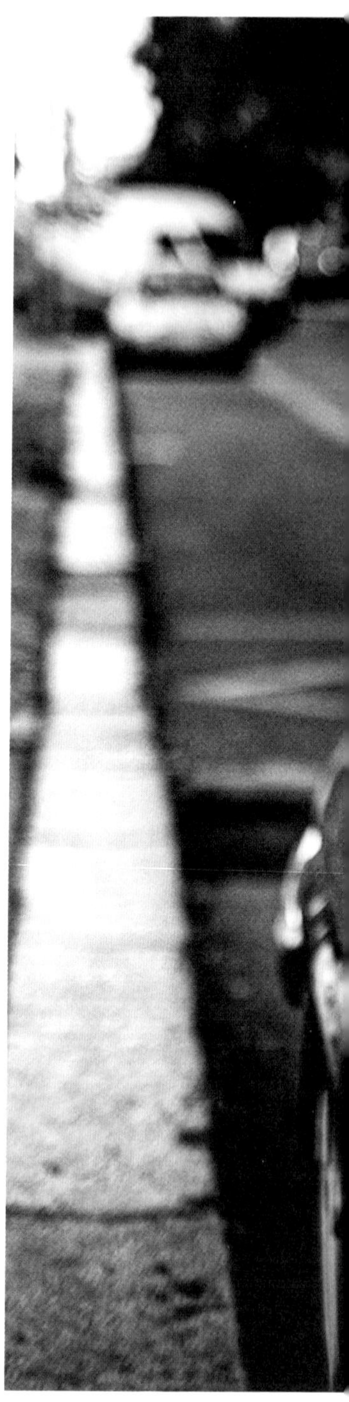

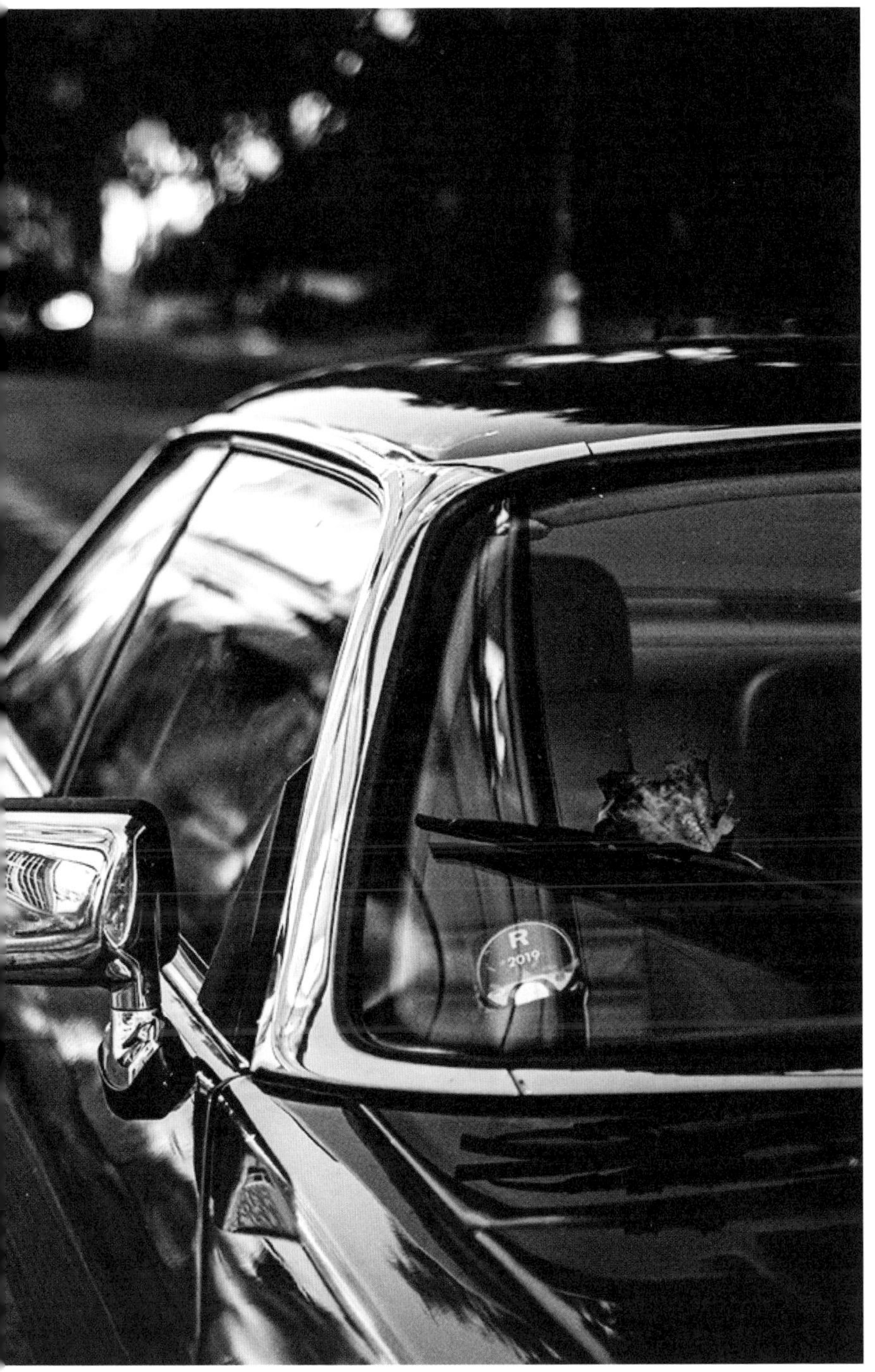
R
2019

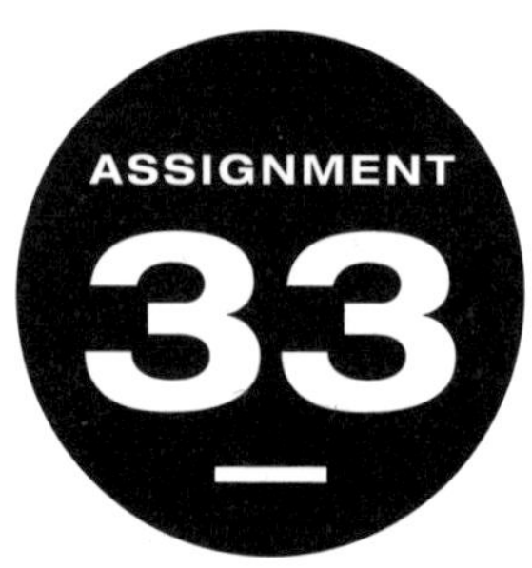

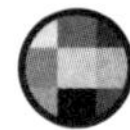

TECHNIQUE

- Keep your eye on the histogram. You're aiming to have most of the information on the left. There shouldn't be any peaks on the right-hand side, although you could have some midtones in the center.
- A quick way to reduce light is to shoot in Aperture Priority mode and dial in -1 or -2 stops on your exposure compensation dial.
- Try using the low-lighting technique called chiaroscuro, an effect originally employed by Renaissance painters, which utilized large areas of darkness in a frame.
- If you're shooting something with a predominantly dark background, make sure the main light source doesn't reach the background.

▶ *The chiaroscuro effect was achieved here by dialing in -2 stops on the exposure compensation dial, resulting in a "headless" man.*

SHOT IN THE DARK

Low-key images contain predominantly dark tones and can convey feelings of mystery, drama, and melancholy. Shadows are used in preference to midtones and highlights, and often become the primary element in the composition.

Your assignment is to create a dramatic low-key image. These techniques can be applied to a wide range of subjects—portraits, product shots, still life, street photography, and landscapes—as well as being used for conceptual abstract images, so let your imagination run free.

Remember, subtlety is the key here: you should be aiming to maximize dark areas and use the minimum of illumination.

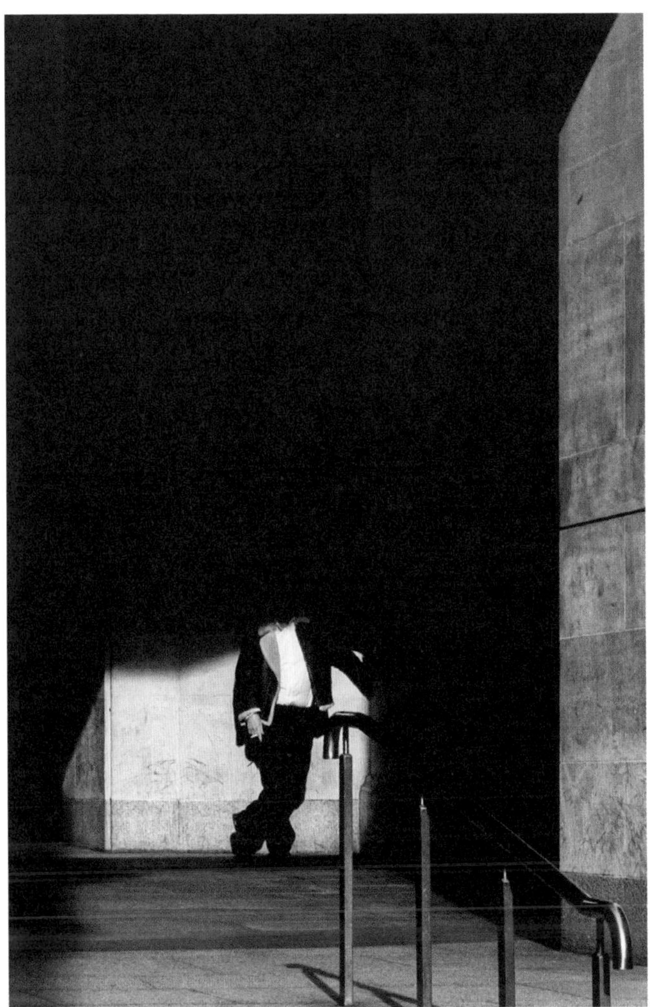

PRO TIPS

- Bear in mind that side lighting is usually more effective than frontal lighting.
- Try shooting using only the light from a candle for a really subtle effect.
- Don't be afraid of having large areas of dark "emptiness" in your image, and use shadow areas to add impact.
- If you can't get the effect you need in-camera, you can make tweaks in post-processing to accentuate dark areas.

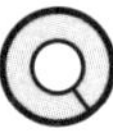

TECHNIQUE

- Shoot in strong sunlight to accentuate contrast and to possibly exaggerate the pattern effect.
- A zoom lens will help you achieve the perfect framing of the pattern.
- Experiment with shooting angles to find the best way to represent your pattern.
- Try to eliminate any distractions that may dilute the effect of the pattern.

► *Try different shooting angles to create the effect you want.*

ASSIGNMENT JOURNAL

PRO TIPS

- Look up! Some of the most interesting patterns appear above our line of sight. Pay attention to architectural detail, tree patterns, and cloud formations, for example.
- Aim for three or more of something to create a pattern.
- Draw out what's important: if the pattern is even, highlight the evenness; if it's broken, make the disruption a feature of your image.
- Remember, you can shoot intangible things, such as shadows (which can make great patterns), as well as physical items.

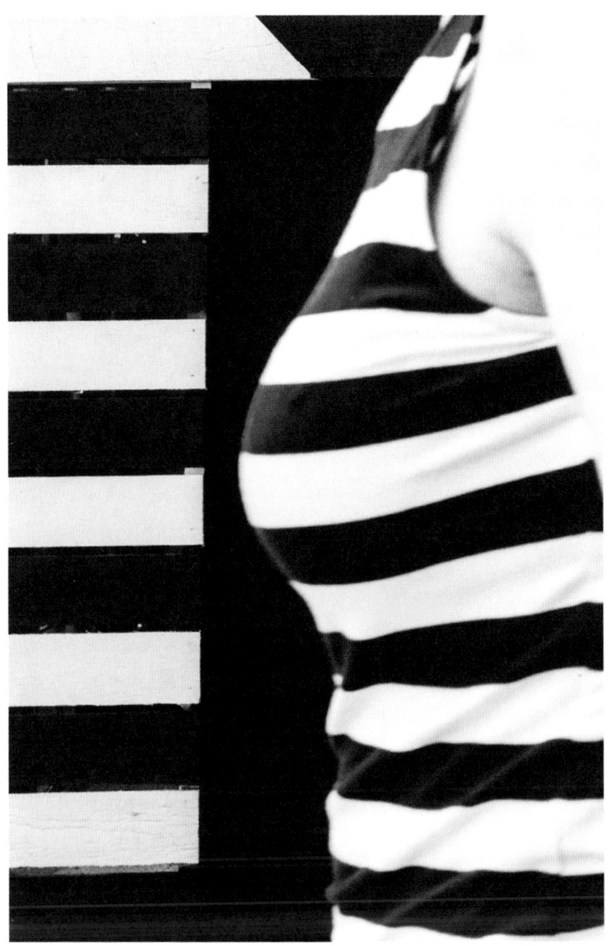

A PATTERN DEVELOPING

We are surrounded by patterns. Regular, irregular, man-made, or naturally occurring, a pattern involves repetition of some kind, and could consist of repeating shapes, lines, objects, colors, buildings, or people, for example. The first part of this assignment is to fire up your powers of observation and find instances of repetition—that's the easy bit!

Now for the main event. Once you've found your pattern, study it and think carefully about how to compose your frame. A good place to start is to fill the whole frame with the pattern, with nothing to distract the eye, which will create a dramatic effect. Alternatively, find some disruption to the pattern, either to cause a visual shock or to deliberately lead the eye out of the frame.

TECHNIQUE

- Make a list of adjectives that imply calmness (soft, light, relaxing, quiet, clear, and easy, for example) and try to incorporate these qualities in your images.
- Slow everything down and take your time. Switch your smartphone off and clear your mind of daily distractions. You'll only produce the sort of images you want if you're in the right state of mind.
- Aim for a smooth tonal range with nothing too "contrasty" or jarring. Overall, bright works better than dark.
- Dial down the clarity and contrast in post-processing. You should be aiming for smoothness and quietness in your images.

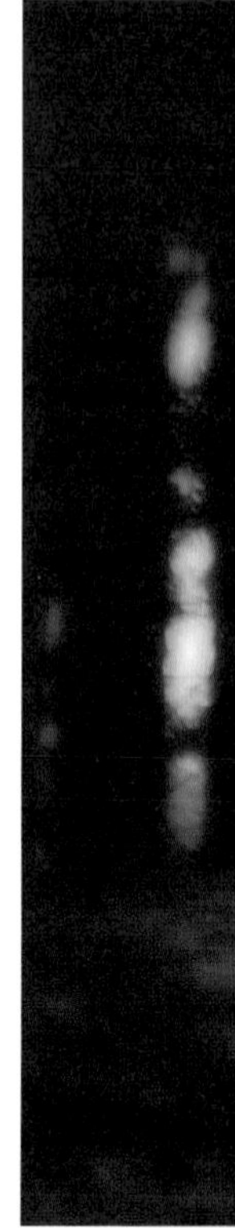

CALM DOWN

With smooth, creamy tones and the right subject, it's not difficult to bring a sense of calm to our black-and-white photography. We all need a little tranquility in our lives, and the aim of this assignment is to shoot an image that, when printed, will induce feelings of relaxation and mindfulness. But there's also another element to this project: as well as creating an image that has a calming effect, your challenge is to bring the art of mindfulness to your picture taking, too.

To complete this assignment, go out with your camera with no agenda and no preconceptions. Try to have an open mind and the attitude that you're going to enjoy yourself, whether you end up taking any good pictures or not.

Whatever you choose to photograph—a landscape, still life, abstract, or a portrait of a loved one—it should be a subject or scene that makes you feel serene.

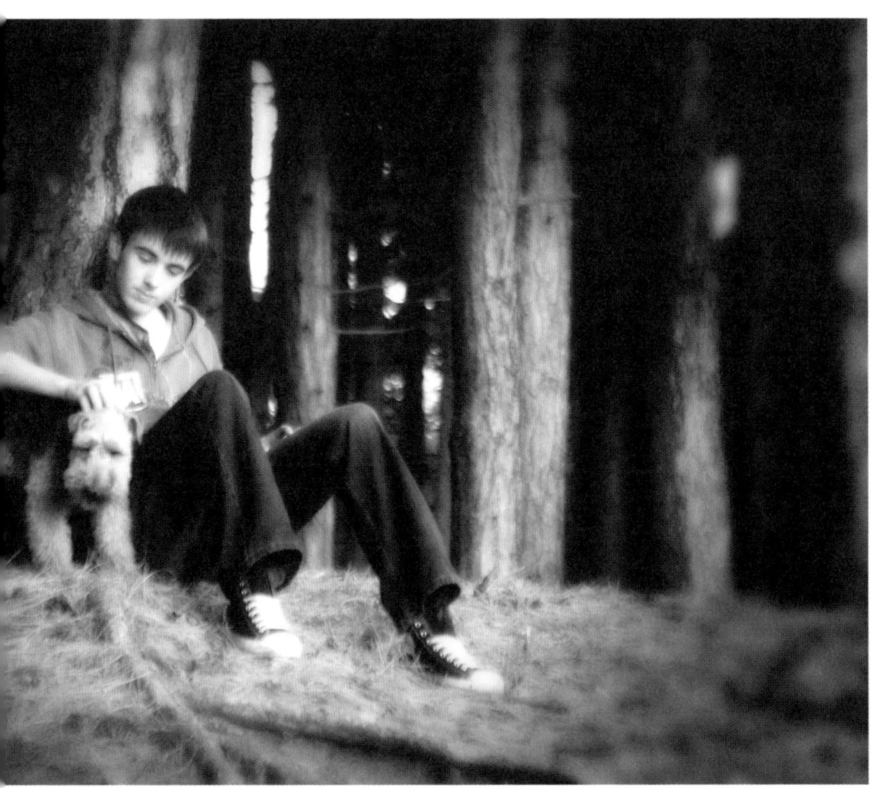

▲ *The ethereal effect in this simple still life was achieved in post-processing by moving the Clarity slider all the way to the left.*

ASSIGNMENT JOURNAL

PRO TIPS

- When you're looking for suitable subjects, don't try too hard. If you overthink it and pressurize yourself into getting the shot, you'll inevitably return home empty-handed.
- Don't get distracted by camera settings and other technical stuff. Switch everything to auto so you can "set it and forget it!"
- If your camera has a Monochrome mode, switch it on so that you'll be seeing the world in black and white.

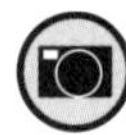

TECHNIQUE

- Shoot in Shutter Priority mode—the key to getting the right amount of blur is having the correct shutter speed. Select a small aperture to prevent overexposure.
- Start with a shutter speed of 1/30 sec. and work your way down from there. Experiment with a range of speeds until you get the effect you want.
- As you'll be using a slow shutter speed, watch out for camera shake. Hold the camera very steady or use a tripod (or lean on something solid, such as a wall) to help you eliminate any movement.

ALL A BLUR

Blur isn't always a bad thing. When used deliberately, it can help to reinforce the illusion of movement in our images. However, creating blur is slightly more difficult in black and white than in color because we have to work harder to create a distinct subject that stands out.

There are two approaches you can take to create a motion blur shot, which is your task for this assignment. You can either capture an image in which the subject is moving, or one where your subject is stationary, while the other things in the frame are in motion. Both methods work and you'll need to choose the one that best suits your subject.

Think about your shutter speed. You'll need to balance the speed of the subject with the ambient light, and finding the correct one will be a case of trial and error. As a rough guide, when photographing people walking at normal speed, you'll need a shutter speed of between 1/8 and 1/30 sec.; for traffic moving at "city" speed, between 1/30 and 1/60 sec.; for a fast-moving subject, such as a train, 1/60 sec.; and for panning shots, between 1/15 and 1/60 sec.

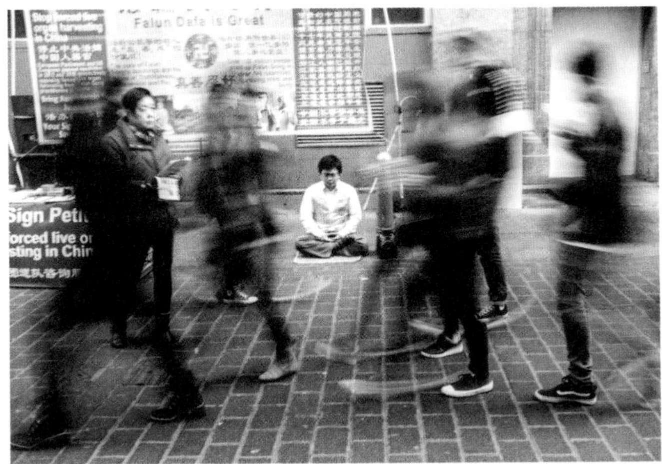

◀ *If you're really careful, and you're not using a heavy lens, it's possible to handhold the camera with a shutter speed of 1/4 sec. and above. (This shot was taken at 1/8 sec.)*

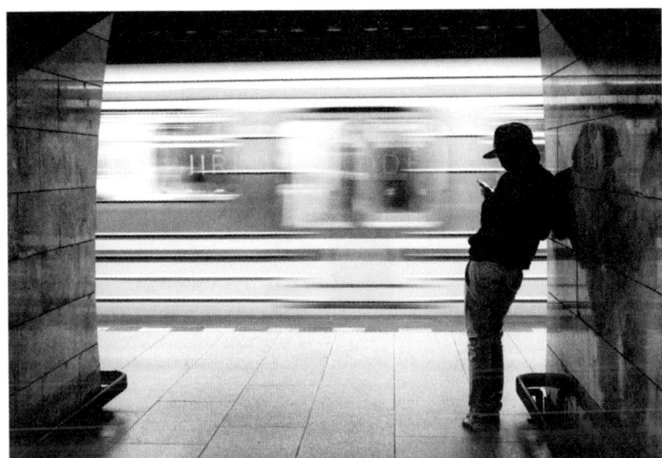

◀ *Fast-moving subjects allow for a faster shutter speed. This train pulling into the station was shot at 1/30 sec.*

PRO TIPS

- It's easy to overexpose with a slow shutter speed if you're shooting in bright conditions, so you'll probably need to keep your ISO at its minimum value. Alternatively, you could use a neutral density (ND) filter.
- A possible, but less interesting option is to create blur in post-processing (Adobe Photoshop, for example, has a Motion Blur filter). Use this option if you missed your shot and need to create blur after the event.
- Try the panning technique (see Assignment 02) to achieve a sharp subject and a dramatic sense of motion in the background.

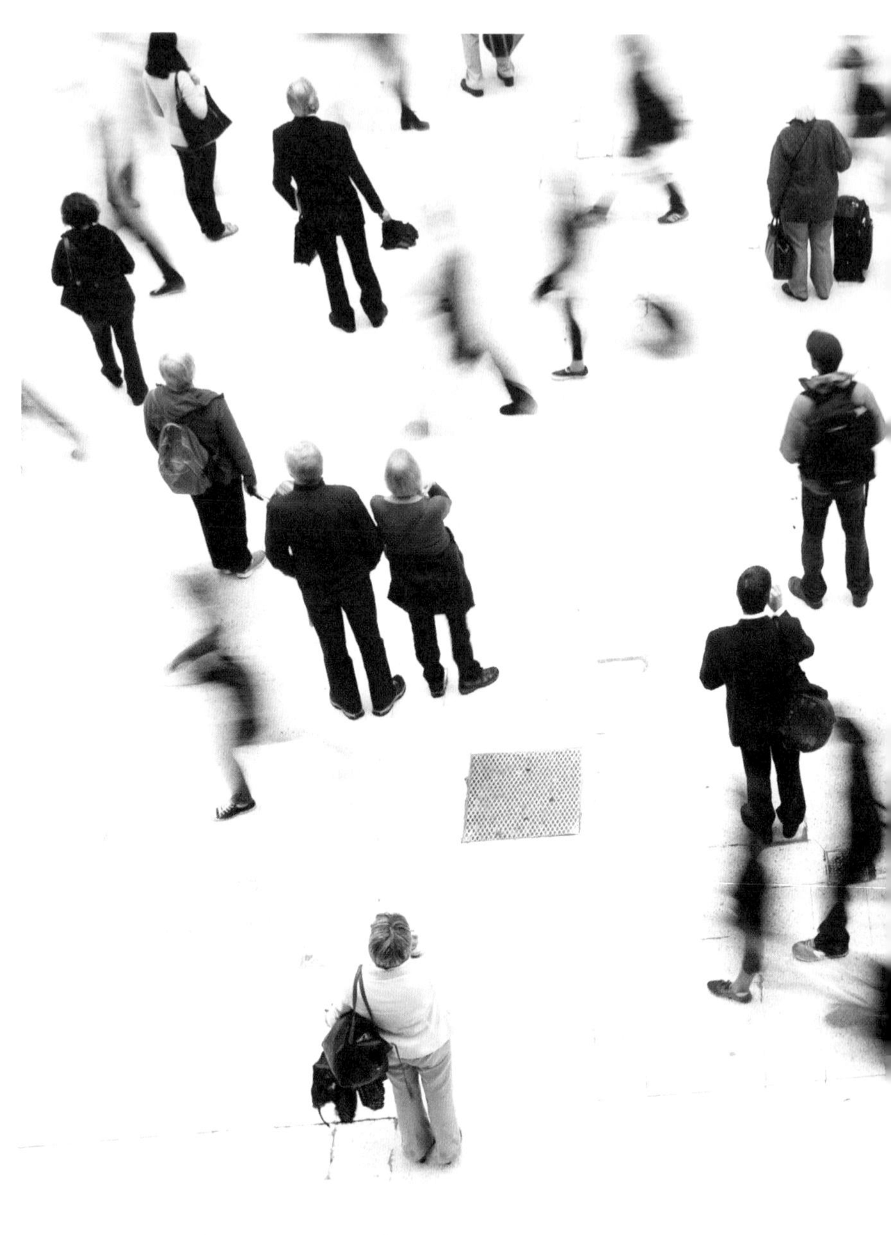

▲ *Resting the camera on the handrail of a balcony, this shot was taken at 1/8 sec., which was just enough to blur the moving people, while ensuring the stationary people remained sharp.*

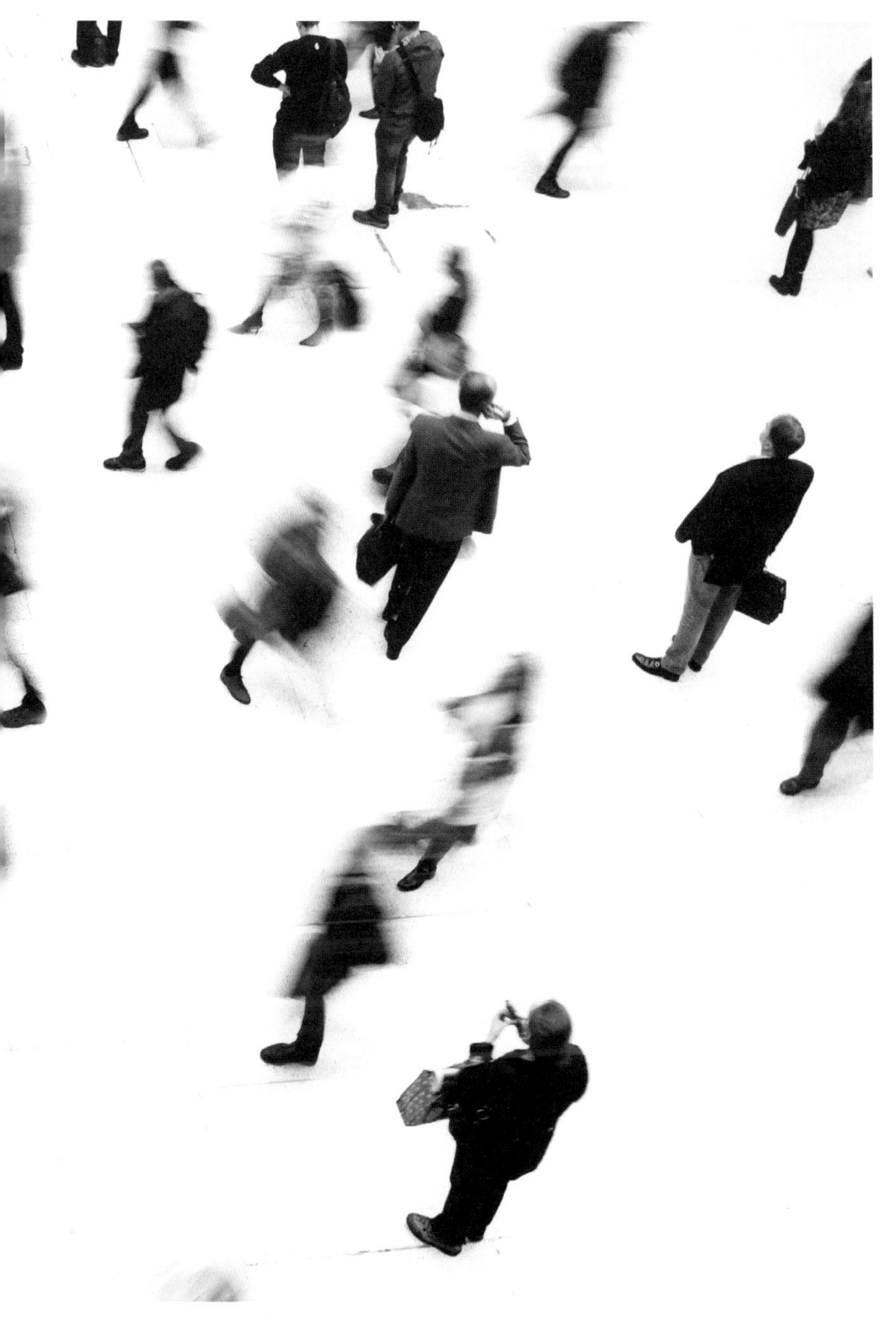

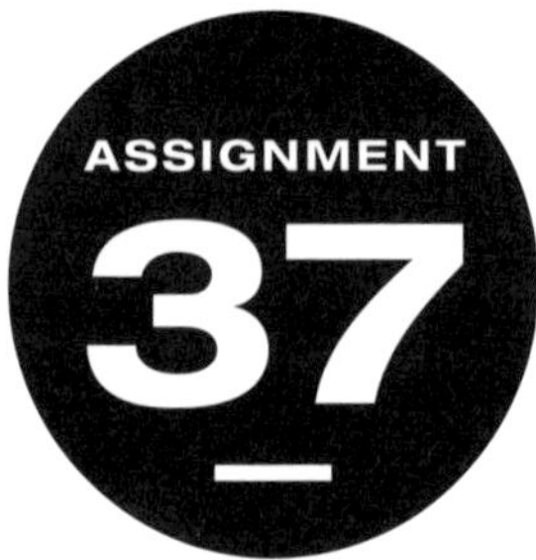

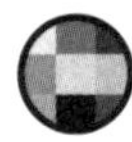

TECHNIQUE

- Use a simple camera setup: set your ISO to auto (letting it go as high as it likes), select Aperture Priority mode, and open up the lens. This combination should give you an acceptably fast shutter speed.
- Avoid using flash whenever possible. It can kill the atmosphere of a night shot.
- Embrace high ISO and accept that there will be some extra noise. In black and white, this can work to your advantage by adding a little atmosphere.
- Find your light source, then stick around and watch the scene around you evolve. At night especially, patience pays off!
- Try a slightly longer lens to isolate detail and create a lovely bokeh effect (see Assignment 42) when wide open—a 50mm or 85mm lens at f/1.4 is perfect.

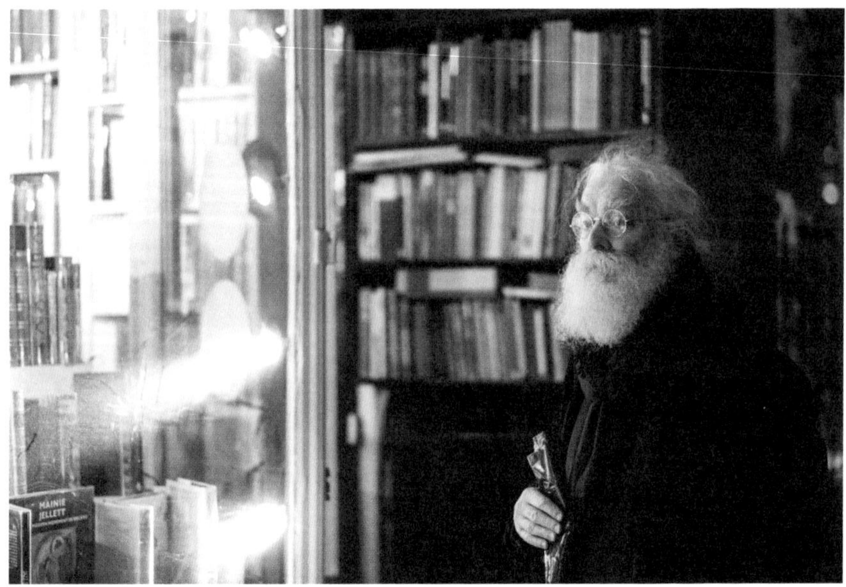

MOTH TO A FLAME

The city streets at night are colorful places with lots of neon lights and vivid reflections. But, if we're shooting in black and white these scenes are more of a challenge, as we can't rely on color to create something interesting. Instead, we have to depend on shapes and, most importantly, the effects of the light.

When shooting after dark we must be more aware than ever of the light, particularly its source, direction, and intensity. Your task here is to shoot an urban scene at night, using a strong light source as a key feature of your image. Try to "think like a moth" and be drawn to the light, the quality of which can make or break your image.

Urban night shooting is often about creating an atmosphere or mood, which could evoke a sense of mystery or intrigue, perhaps. Rather than giving the viewer all the answers immediately, it's sometimes best to hold something back, allowing them the opportunity to form their own conclusions about, for example, what's behind that door or who's at that window.

And remember, dark means dark! You should bear in mind that digital cameras have a habit of brightening nighttime shots, so if you're using Aperture Priority mode (see left), simply use the exposure compensation setting to dial in a stop or two of underexposure.

PRO TIPS

- Go easy in post-processing and make local rather than global adjustments.
- Shoot in Raw so that any unwanted noise can be eliminated easily in post-processing later on.
- Take extra care at night and be very aware of who's around you and what they're doing.

◀ *A store window can offer the ideal light source. Sometimes, when you find a great light source, it's worth waiting around for the right subject to come into the frame.*

ASSIGNMENT JOURNAL

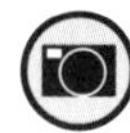

TECHNIQUE

- Set your camera to shoot both Raw and Jpeg images (most modern cameras will allow you to do this). Then, set the Jpeg to Monochrome (your Raw file will be unaffected). Assuming your camera has a Live View function, you'll now be seeing the world in black and white, which will help you make a more informed composition.
- Get into the habit of going out with the intention of shooting in monochrome. Don't use black and white as an emergency option to resuscitate an otherwise boring color shot.
- Try wearing sunglasses with brown or amber lenses. These will reduce your vision to a much more monochromatic view, which can provide a good guide for tonality and contrast.

HOW TO "SEE" IN BLACK AND WHITE

1. The first stage is recognition. Start off by looking for simple compositions and strong graphic shapes. Study compositional elements that don't rely on color for impact.
2. Think about contrast. Study the tonal range of a scene and see where light meets dark. You should seek out situations with strong contrast.
3. Next, consider the direction and intensity of the light. Light and shade add depth and dimension as they hit the edges and contours of your subject. Work out how the subject changes under different lighting conditions.
4. Think about tonal range. You'll want deep blacks, bright whites, and a wide range of gray shades in between. This wide tonal range will result in an image that's much more interesting than a flat picture full of midtones.
5. Finally, think about how colors will work alongside each other when viewed in black and white. Again, you're looking for contrast and separation rather than many similar tones, so study a little color theory to see how colors relate to one another.

A NEW VISION

Having black and white "vision" is critical if you're going to make this medium a success. Think of it as learning a new language or a whole new way of seeing the world. The black-and-white world is one in which form, shape, contrast, luminosity, pattern, and texture all become more important without the distraction of color.

This assignment is less about taking pictures and more about becoming so familiar with that new "language" that it becomes second nature. It's really an exercise in pre-visualization (the ability to know what will work well in black and white, and what won't), and a big part of this is simply training your eyes and brain to work in a new way.

The only equipment you'll need for this assignment is your eyes. Follow the steps (below left) and undertake this exercise as many times as you can without a camera. Then, when it comes to taking pictures, you should find that you have much stronger visualization skills.

▼ *Your first consideration should always be contrast. You'll want to strive for punchy blacks and bright whites, resulting in good tonal separation.*

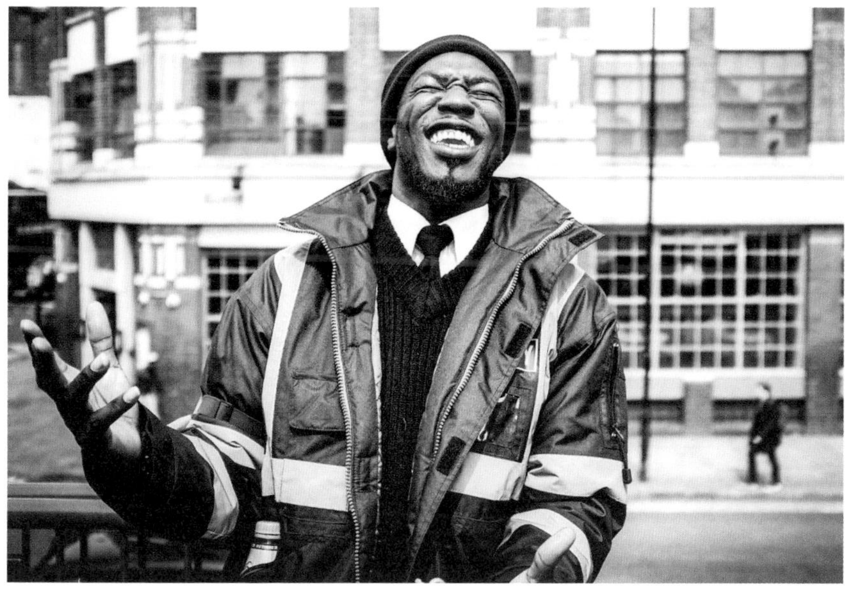

TECHNIQUE

- Try to get a good variety of subject matter in your project: people, buildings, vistas, objects, activities, and so on.
- Context is crucial here. Always think about stepping back to include some all-important background information.
- You don't need a lot of equipment for this assignment, just a camera and a few lenses (covering the range 35–85mm is ideal). It's fine to use flash, but natural light is easier to manage and will help you to convey a "documentary" feel.
- Don't overdo it in post-processing. This genre is all about authenticity, so overprocessed or manipulated images are frowned upon.

ASSIGNMENT JOURNAL

PRO TIPS

- Don't direct your scenes. Documentary photography is about reality and you should create a truthful representation of what is in front of you.
- Get to know the people who will feature in your pictures. This familiarity will help to produce a natural and relaxed result.
- If you produce a small photobook or zine (see Assignment 28), you could try selling it through the local bookstore or gallery.
- Be prepared to modify your concept during the project.

IN THE 'HOOD

Documentary photography has always been closely associated with the medium of black and white. Perhaps this is because it's easier to tell a story without the distraction of color, or it could be something to do with nostalgia. Whatever the reason, a lot of great black-and-white documentary work has been created around the concept of the neighborhood. Most of us live in a neighborhood of some sort and that local community is what you'll be focusing on in this assignment.

Some excellent examples of previous neighborhood documentary projects include: a work by a photographer who, after 45 years, revisited the street in which he was born and photographed every resident; a project that focused on how social issues such as drug abuse and anti-social behavior have impacted on a neighborhood; and a collecton of images of neighbors and their pets—a "pawtrait" of a local community.

Remember that the objective of any documentary exercise is good storytelling. You should have a well-formed idea of your story and be prepared to explain it to others. Choose a theme, spend some time developing your idea, then start shooting. Aim for between 24 and 36 final images and remember that sequencing is critical: every story has a beginning, a middle, and an end, and the flow of images through the project should reflect this.

▼ *Documentary pictures needn't feature people; you can often get your message across in other ways.*

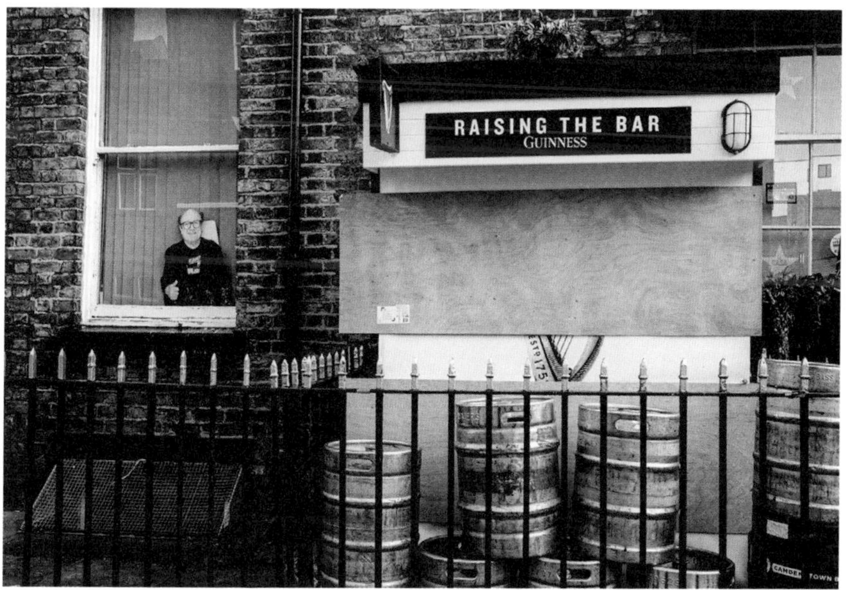

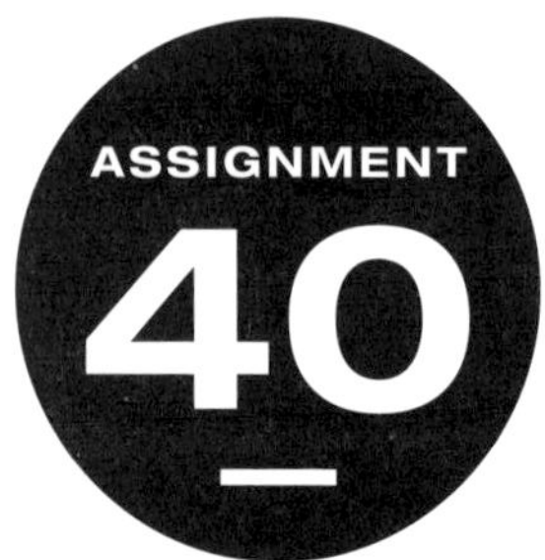

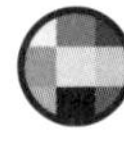

TECHNIQUE

- Choose the right lens for the effect you want: a long lens will make the fog appear more dense and a wideangle will minimize its impact.
- Switch to manual focus, as the auto focus will find it difficult to focus on a target. Focus on foreground elements to add a sense of depth.
- Getting the right exposure can be tricky, so it's often worth bracketing a few stops to get it spot on.
- Use a tripod or a high ISO, as the scene may be darker than it looks.
- Use a small aperture to retain some definition in your picture.

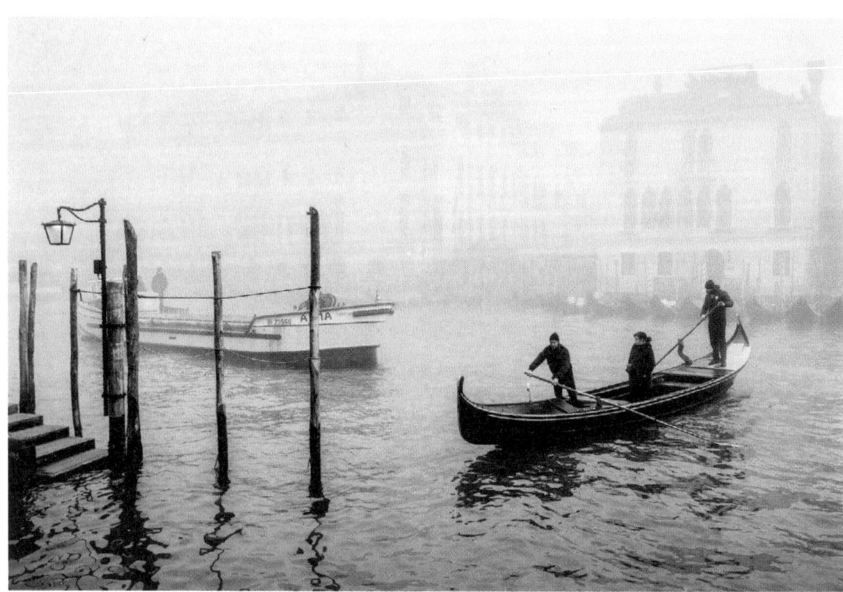

OUT OF THE GLOOM

Ethereal and atmospheric, fog is one of those subjects that is perfectly suited to being shot in black and white. Acting as a giant diffuser, it flattens out tones and often produces an eerie glow.

However, whether you're shooting a landscape, an ocean view, or an urban scene, the resulting image can sometimes bear no resemblance to what you are seeing in front of you. So, for this assignment, your task is to create a striking, evocative image of fog that accurately represents your chosen scene.

The good news is that you needn't wait for thick fog—even a gentle mist will work well—and you can create something just as impactful in your own street as in any exotic location.

PRO TIPS

- Keep an eye on your lens filter (or front element) and check for condensation. Also, resist the temptation to change lenses in thick fog; it's bad news when moist air gets anywhere near your sensor.
- Get out of bed early! Early-morning mist and fog in the fall is great for creating timeless, evocative street scenes. Aim to be outside around 15–30 minutes after sunrise.
- For some spectacular effects, look out for light rays as the sun is making its appearance.
- Some subtle toning in post-processing can add to the drama—blue and yellow work well.

ASSIGNMENT JOURNAL

◀ *Strong foreground interest can increase the sense of depth in a shot that has lingering fog in the background, particularly when using a shallowish depth of field (f/5.6 in this case).*

TECHNIQUE

- Simplify your settings: Aperture Priority, f/8, 1/250 sec., and Auto ISO should work well.
- Use zone (manual) focusing so you won't need to worry about where your point of focus is.
- Prime lenses are less obtrusive—a 24mm and 50mm would be ideal.
- Aim to shoot quickly and confidently, without hesitation.

▼ *Some protests are much calmer than others, though you'll generally feel safer and more comfortable if you're surrounded by police officers.*

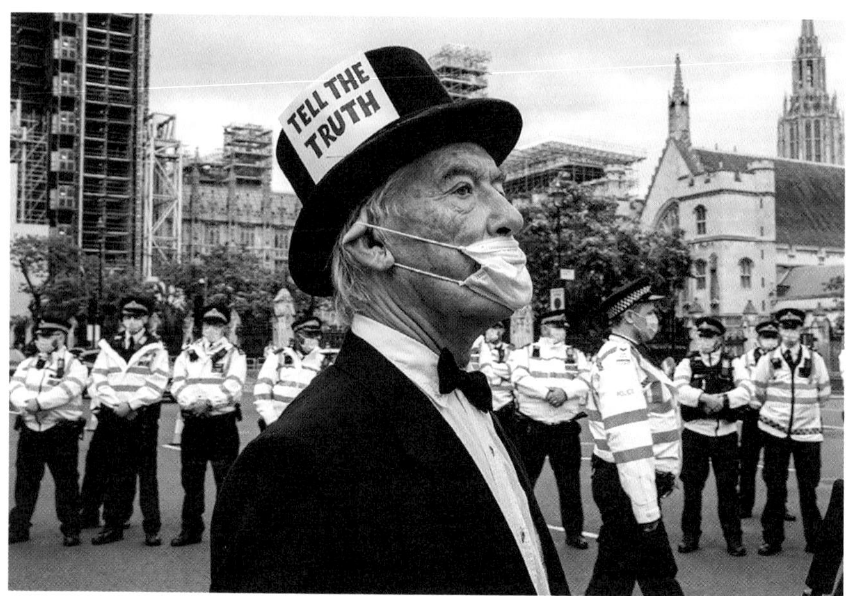

TAKE TO THE STREETS

In this "age of unrest," you'll probably find protests, marches, or demonstrations happening not far from where you live, wherever you are in the world. Protests attract photographers like bees to a honeypot, but many of them shoot without any sort of plan or purpose. For this assignment, your job is to attend a protest of some kind and create a short photoessay that documents the event.

This type of assignment lends itself perfectly to the black-and-white medium and you need look no further than the work of Don McCullin or some of the Magnum photographers for inspiration. But before you start shooting, think about the story you want to tell: will it be politically or socially motivated? Will it be humorous? Will it feature the main event or fringe activities? As with a written essay, you need to plan your story first.

Imagine your set of images as a story of eight to ten pictures in a Sunday newspaper supplement. Aim for one headline (or "hero") picture, with the rest of the photographs telling the story from beginning to end.

PRO TIPS

Protests can be quite unpredictable, so you'll need to keep your wits about you. Follow these safety guidelines to stay safe and enjoy the experience:

- Bring a buddy. You'll feel and be safer if there are two of you.
- Be respectful and don't get too close to people's faces.
- Try to shoot in places where there are lots of police officers around you.
- Take as little kit as possible. Leave expensive watches, jewelry, and other valuables at home. Don't take anything you can't afford to lose.
- If you're challenged while taking someone's photo, smile, thank them, and walk away. Most of the time, this will diffuse the situation. If someone insists that you delete an image, do so.
- Have good situational awareness—know what's going on around you at all times.
- Always know your way out (escape route), and decide on a meeting point if you're shooting with others.
- Try to blend in. Don't dress or behave like a photographer, or look out of place in any way. Ideally, wear dark clothing and don't carry a photographer's bag.

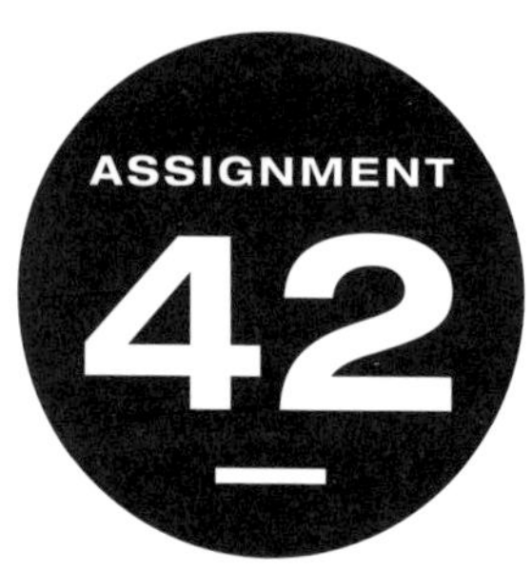

TECHNIQUE

- The starting point for bokeh is a wide aperture. Anything wider than f/2.8 should work, but the wider the better.
- The more distance between your subject and the background, the stronger the bokeh effect will be (this is useful if you don't have a fast lens). A longer lens will also give you the potential for more bokeh.
- If you like big light "orbs" in your bokeh, experiment with different lenses, focal lengths, and apertures, as each one of these will give different characteristics.
- As a last resort, you can create a bokeh effect in post-processing, but it feels like cheating!

BIG BOKEH

Bokeh (pronounced bow-ke) comes from the Japanese word "boke," which means "haze" or "blur." It refers to the soft, out-of-focus background you get when shooting with a fast lens at a wide aperture, usually f/2.8 or wider.

While you can incorporate the bokeh effect into many types of photography—still life, nature, landscape, abstract—it works particularly well with portraits, helping to separate the subject from the background. The purpose of this assignment is to familiarize yourself with the concept of shooting wide open to create bokeh, so that you can incorporate it into your photography more generally. Your task is to shoot four images using this technique: a portrait; a landscape; a nighttime street shot; and an abstract, in which the bokeh itself is the subject.

Make bokeh part of your thinking for all subjects and you'll bring so much more variety to your black-and-white photography.

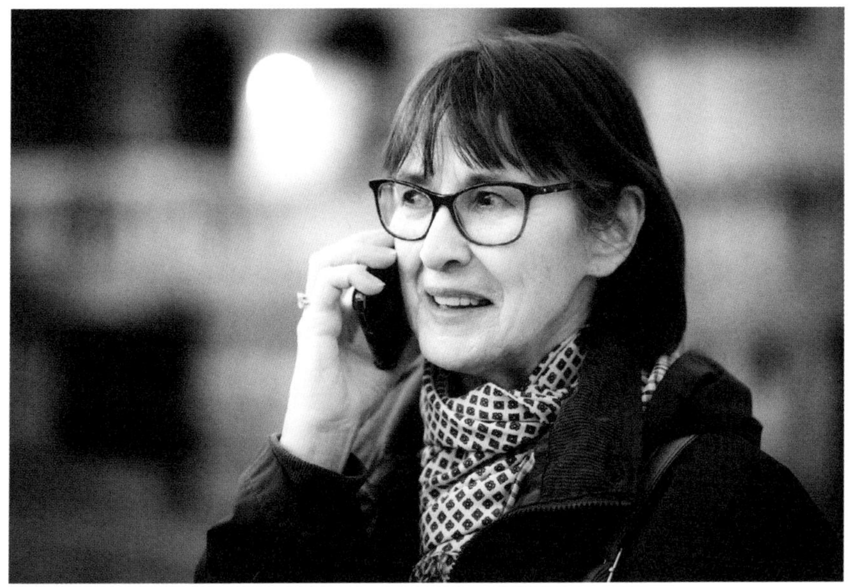

▲ *Portrait: There's no better way to draw attention to a face than to have a "bokeh-licious" background.*

PRO TIPS

- Your bokeh effect doesn't need to be the background. It could just as easily be the foreground.
- This is a great technique to try at night, especially with lots of twinkling lights in the background.
- Different lenses will represent bokeh in different ways. Get to know the characteristics of each lens so that you can exploit its creativity.
- You can use bokeh strategically to hide or disguise unwanted elements in a composition.

ASSIGNMENT JOURNAL

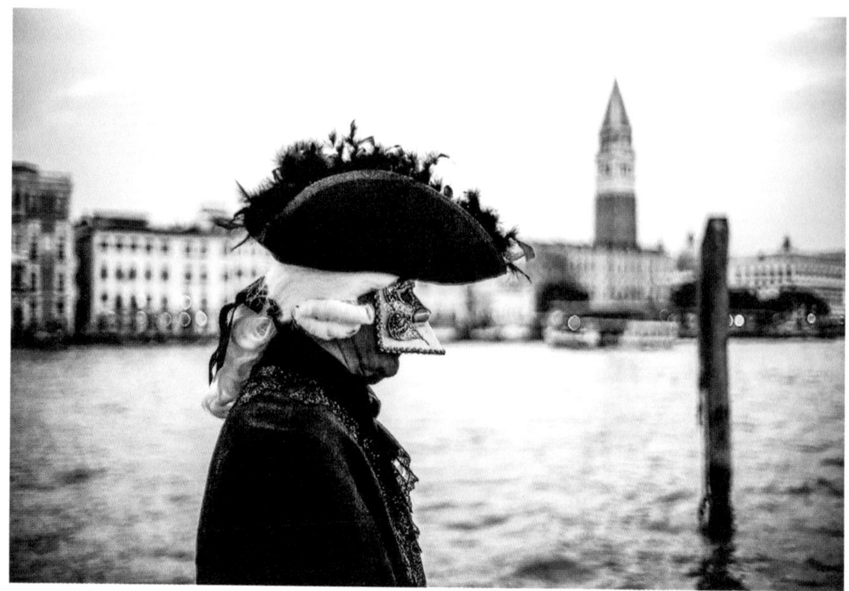

▲ *Landscape: The landscape element here is actually the bokeh, but the shot works because the out-of-focus area is a recognizable landmark.*

▼ *Abstract: If your image has lots of light "orbs," use the Color Mixer sliders in post-processing to highlight some and de-emphasize others.*

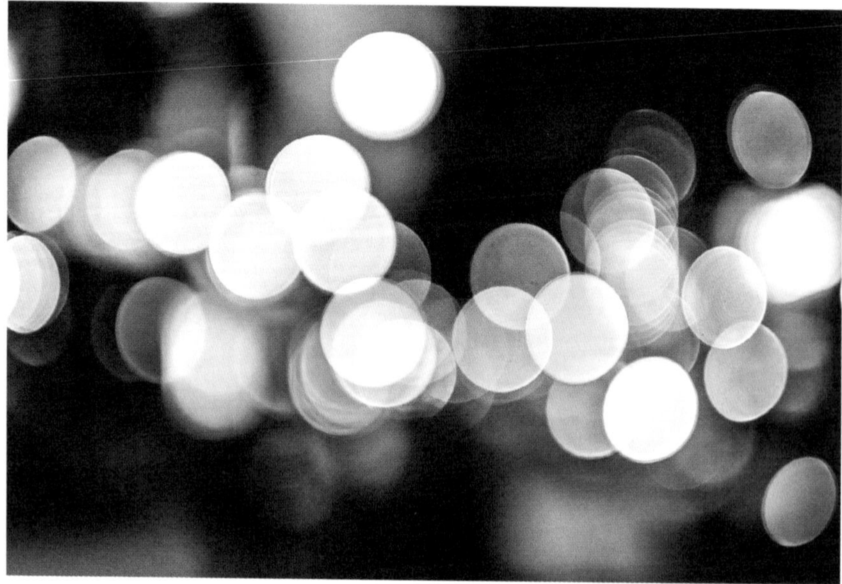

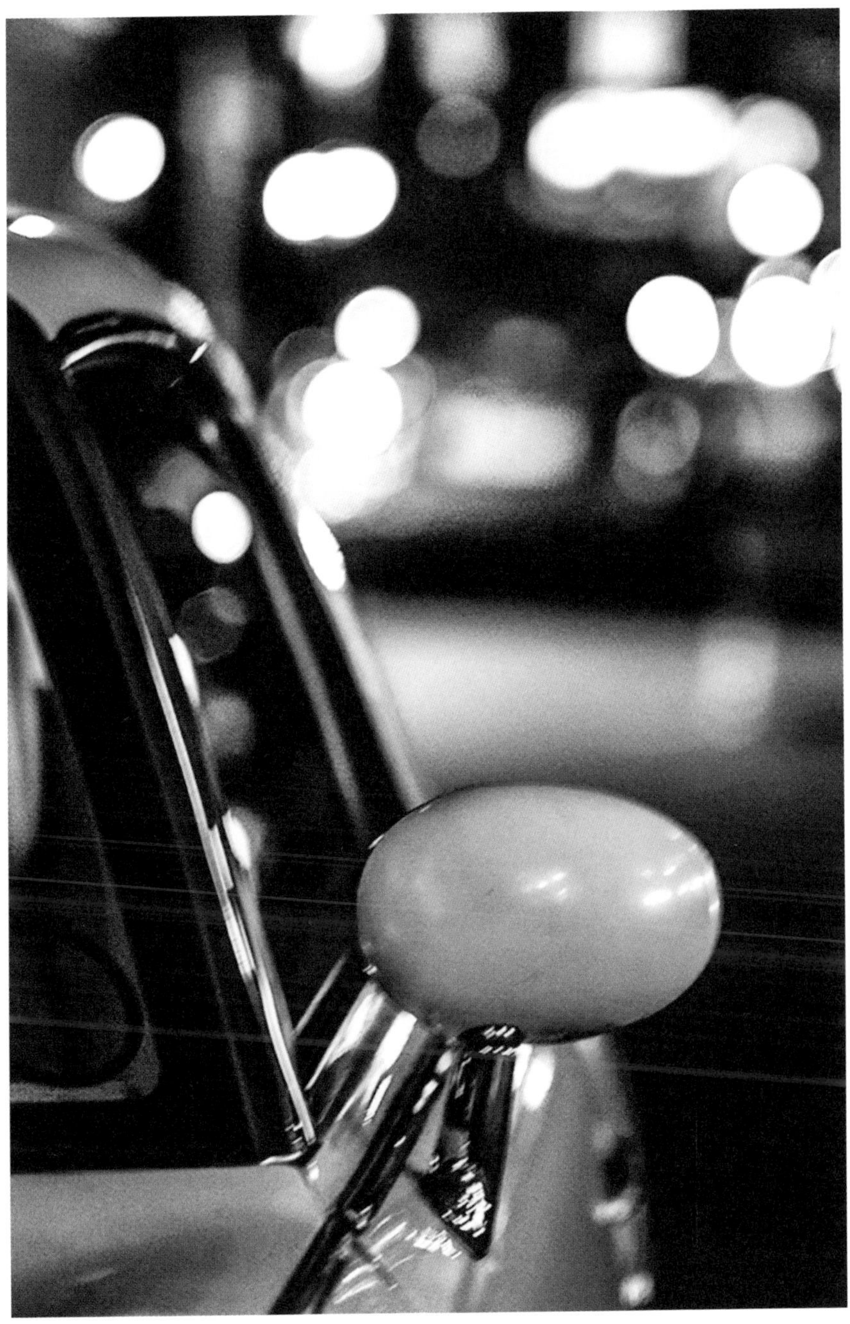

▲ *Nighttime street: It's great fun to experiment with bokeh at night, especially in a town or city where there is a variety of light sources.*

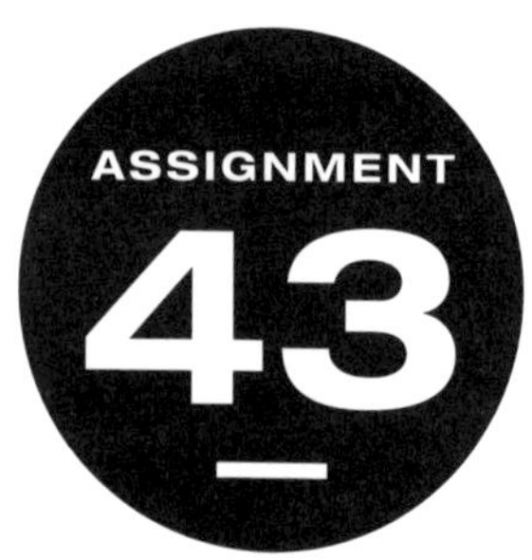

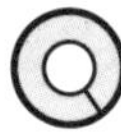

TECHNIQUE

- A longer lens will be helpful, as it will allow you to isolate detail that may otherwise be inaccessible—a 70–200mm zoom would be ideal.
- Although it's often not essential when capturing detail, you may want to straighten up some of the lines. You could try using the perspective correction tools in your image-editing software to correct any perspective distortion.
- Get to "know" the building. Walk around it, exploring all the angles and noticing how it's affected by different light conditions.
- Use a polarizing filter to avoid unwanted reflections in your images.

BUILDING DETAIL

We tend to view buildings as a whole, enjoying the wider vista and ignoring the opportunities to be found in the details. Old or new, brutalist or Gothic, every building is a sum of smaller parts, and the basis of this assignment is to use those parts to create some striking images.

This is an exercise in isolation and, ultimately, "seeing." Buildings contain a great number of intricate details, which can be lost when we shoot the facade in one frame. Getting up close could tell a different story, however, revealing something new about the building's history, for example.

Explore your chosen building from every conceivable angle, experimenting with different focal lengths to get the desired composition.

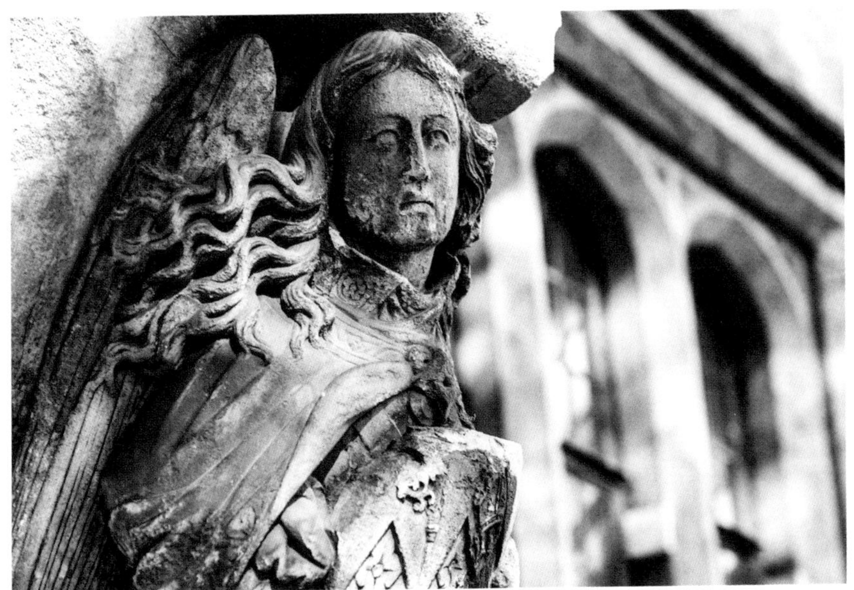

▲ *Texture can be an interesting feature of ancient aspects like this, and a long lens will help you close in on the detail.*

PRO TIPS

- Consider using strong graphical elements to create an abstract image. These could be exaggerated with dramatic lighting.
- To help bring out the shape and texture of the subject, look for situations where the light hits the detail at an angle.
- A tripod or monopod will allow you to use a slower shutter speed and therefore a lower ISO, which is very helpful when shooting interior detail.
- If you have three images of similar subject matter, try grouping them together to make a triptych.

ASSIGNMENT JOURNAL

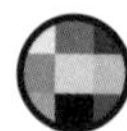

TECHNIQUE

- Use Aperture Priority mode and select the aperture according to your depth of field requirement.
- Dial in -1 stop of exposure compensation to start with, then review and adjust as required. The amount of compensation you need will depend on how bright the sun is compared to the light falling on your subject.
- Remember that exposure compensation doesn't work in Manual mode. If you prefer shooting manually, use your combination of aperture, shutter speed, and ISO to manually select an exposure that works for your scene and desired effect.
- You can choose to combat flare or embrace it. To eliminate flare, shoot when the sun is higher in the sky and use a lens hood, or cup your hand around the front of the lens. Alternatively, enjoy the effect and shoot right into the light!

INTO THE LIGHT

By shooting directly into bright light, you can create highlights and shadows without much in between. This is often referred to as contre-jour photography, meaning "against daylight," and is something photographers are generally taught to avoid when they're starting out. However, once you've confidently mastered the technique you'll be unstoppable.

When it comes to exposure, there are two approaches for contre-jour shooting: you can overexpose to retain detail in the shadows, or you can underexpose for a more impactful effect. In this assignment, you'll be doing the latter, aiming to create a dramatic image with deep shadows and sparkling light.

Your brief is to head out on a bright, sunny day to find a scene that interests you and has the sun behind it. Get the exposure right and you should achieve a striking, stylish image.

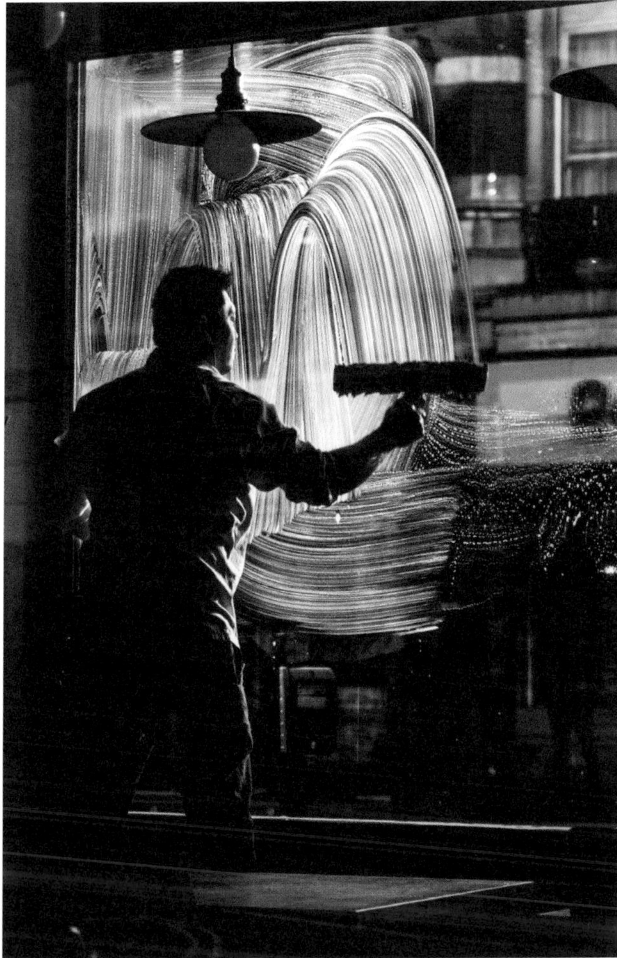

◀ *Direct sunlight streaming into your lens is good, but not essential. Here, the sun is out of shot but it illuminates the window perfectly.*

PRO TIPS

- Shoot when the sun is low for dramatic results. You'll get increased flare and long shadows.
- If you need to shoot quickly, just keep the mantra "expose for the highlights" in mind and you won't go far wrong.
- You can regulate the amount of flare by changing your viewpoint to position your subject in front of the sun.
- Most prime lenses will handle flare better than zooms, mainly because of their less complex element groupings.

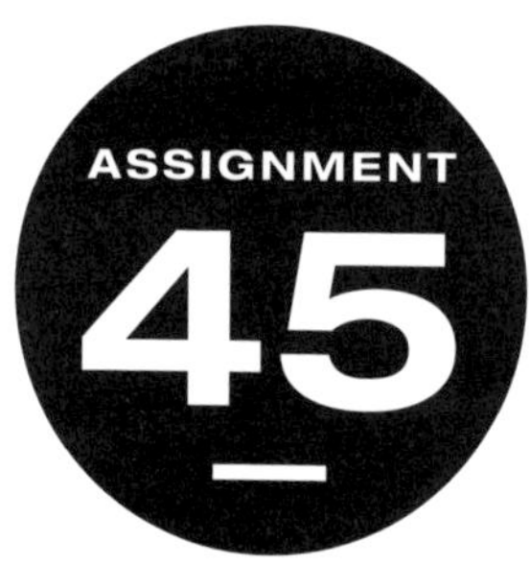

TECHNIQUE

- Be instinctive: shoot what you see and shoot it quickly.
- Add an extra element of imperfection in post-processing by increasing the contrast.
- Don't worry about noise (or grain) and whack up your ISO—try 1600 or 3200.

PRO TIPS

- This style is very well suited to street scenes, especially in busy places where there's plenty of movement and energy.
- Try shooting this project at nighttime; darkness can add great atmosphere.
- Very cheap or vintage lenses have their own "built-in" imperfections, especially at their widest setting, and can offer a good starting point.

PERFECTLY IMPERFECT

From our earliest endeavors in photography, most of us are taught to strive for perfection: lines must be straight, grain should be nonexistent, the Rule of Thirds is sacrosanct, and so on. And, for much of what we do, this works very well. If you're a landscape, fashion, or product photographer, for example, perfection is your friend. However, for many of us, it could be seen as a constraint, holding us back and strangling our creativity.

Your challenge here is to embrace imperfection. You'll need to throw all notions of perfection out of the window and shoot fast and loose, with fluidity and passion. Take a leaf out of Daido Moriyama's book, the great Japanese street photographer, whose fabulous monochrome images were often grainy, soft, or oddly composed, but had real energy.

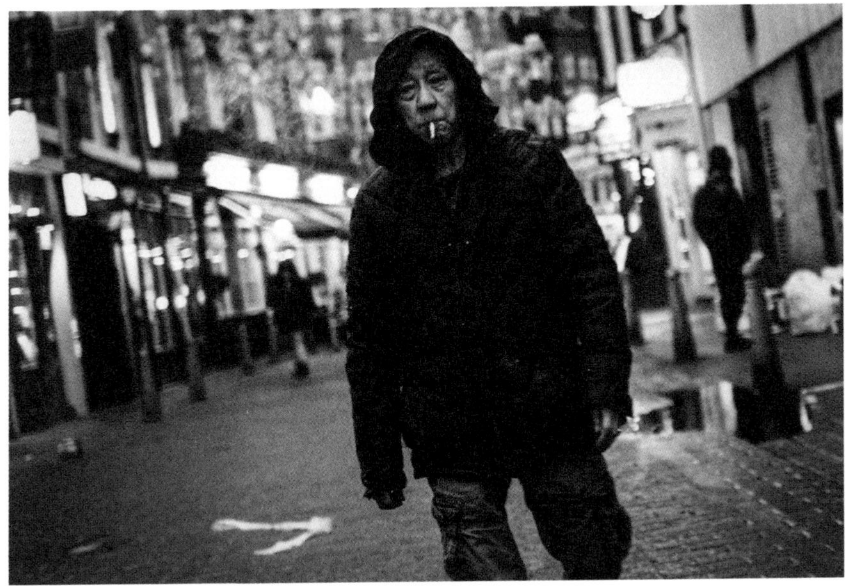

▲ *Don't obsess about neatness or "correct" angles. Unusual compositions can add a welcome sense of tension.*

▼ *You could use reflections to add an extra layer and to bring a little extra chaos to the composition.*

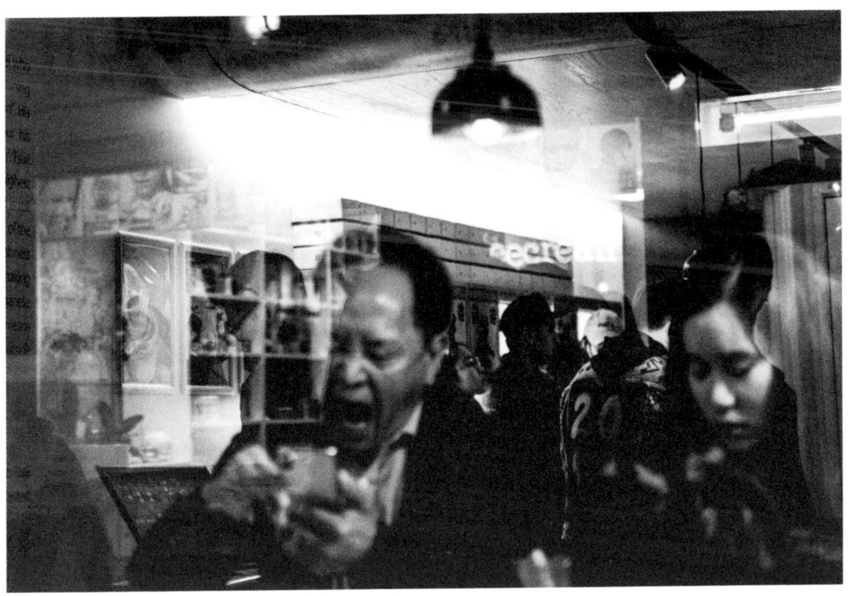

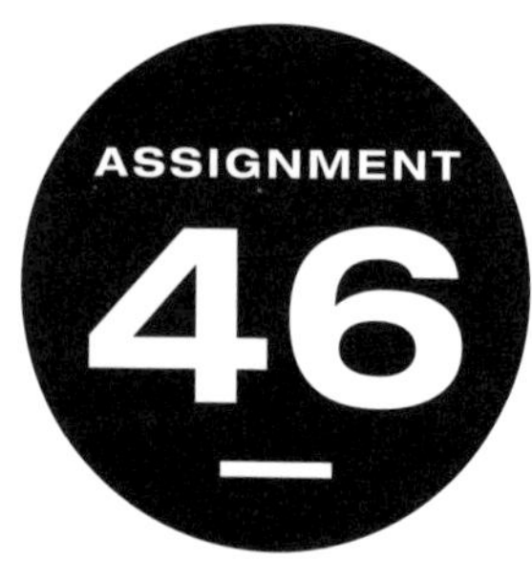

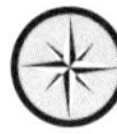

TECHNIQUE

- Shoot with a purpose: look for focal points and interesting features.
- Bracket your exposure, especially in the harsh light of summer, and err on the side of underexposure to keep the highlights in check.
- Use your filters. A UV filter will reduce atmospheric haze and will keep sand away from your precious glass. A polarizer will help reduce reflections and boost contrast.
- Flare isn't always a bad thing (see Assignment 44). Consider using it creatively to add atmosphere.
- Make sure the horizon is straight, as even a slightly crooked skyline can ruin your shot.

LIFE'S A BEACH

Most of us have access to a beach, whether we live locally to one or make an annual pilgrimage to the shore. The great thing about beaches is they're an excellent place to practice some black-and-white shooting skills.

For this assignment, your task is to shoot a collection of beach photographs based around a theme, rather than shooting lots of random images. You could choose to focus on the ocean—crashing waves, windblown sands, and cloud formations—or people, perhaps experimenting with a social documentary approach, à la Martin Parr. The weather is another option, as beaches are usually exposed and attract dramatic conditions. You could revisit a specific beach at different times throughout the year or capture a collection of objects found while beachcombing.

Whatever your theme, use this assignment to take your creativity for a walk along the beach and come home with a bucketload of great shots.

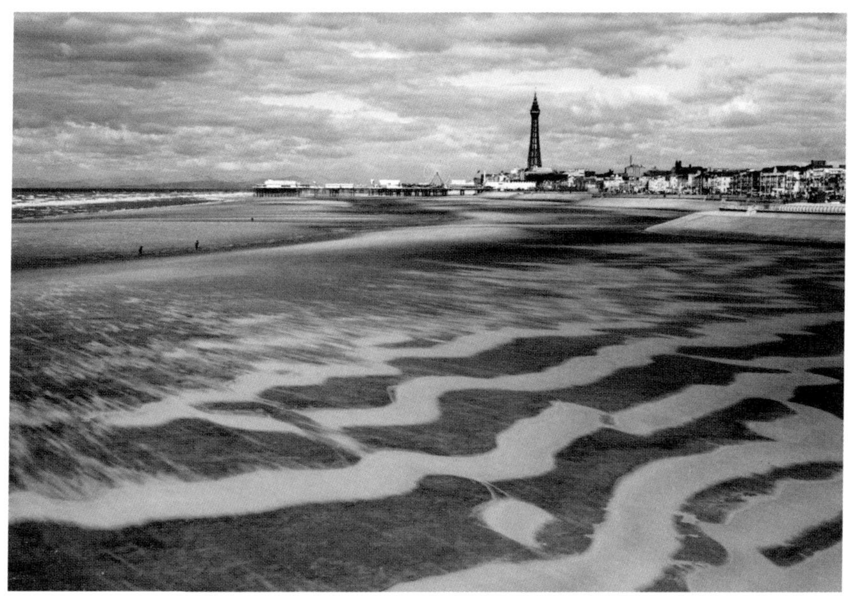

▲ *Look out for interesting patterns and textures on the beach, especially on a windy day when the sand gets blown into troughs like these.*

PRO TIPS

- Choose quieter times when you can shoot without clutter and make more thoughtful compositions.
- Don't let bad weather inhibit you! Dark, stormy days are ideal for beach photography, especially early or late in the day.
- If you're shooting on a busy beach, be prepared to explain yourself to others, as your motives could easily be misconstrued.

ASSIGNMENT JOURNAL

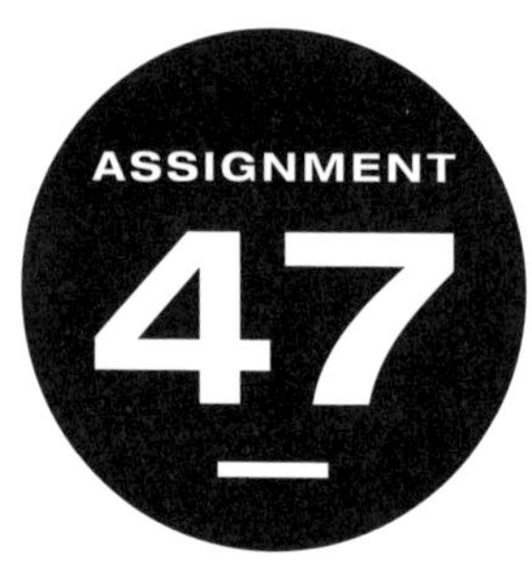

TECHNIQUE

- Choose an object that will offer you lots of variety and plenty of angles to explore.
- Plan your images before you start shooting. The first few ideas should come easily, but you'll need to get creative to complete a strong list of nine variations.
- Experiment with different light types, sources, and directions. Small tweaks can make significant differences.
- High-contrast images will work better than "flat" ones, so don't be afraid of punchy blacks and bright whites.
- Try to visualize how the nine images will work together as the finished project, possibly in a uniform grid of square-framed prints.

NINE WAYS

This is a fun assignment designed to test your versatility and get your creative juices flowing. Your brief is to find an object you're fond of and photograph it in nine different ways. Try to choose an object you have a deep personal connection with and don't just photograph it from different angles. Shoot it in different scenarios, under different lighting conditions, and in unusual situations.

Before you begin, spend some time thinking through your concepts and making notes. An initial list of ideas for this example (a treasured vintage SLR camera) included: on a tripod; close-up detail; selfie; abstract; surrounded by film; in its bag; moody lighting; out of context; and as part of a flat lay (shot from directly above).

Other than shooting nine photographs, so that you can display the resulting images in a grid, there are no rules. Allow your imagination to run wild—the wackier the shots, the better!

▶ *This vintage SLR camera offered plenty of scope for imaginative shots (continued on pages 114–15).*

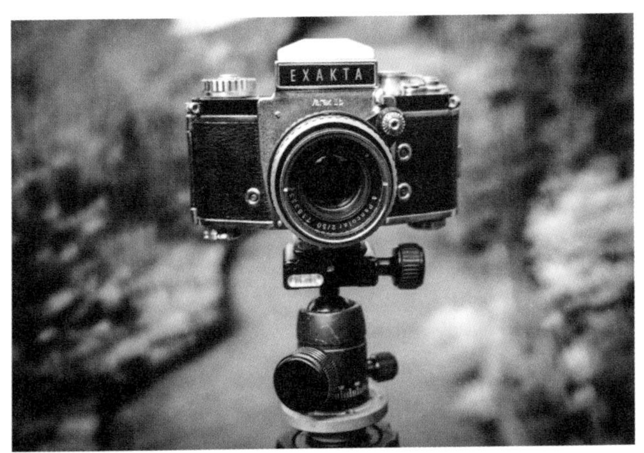
EXAKTA

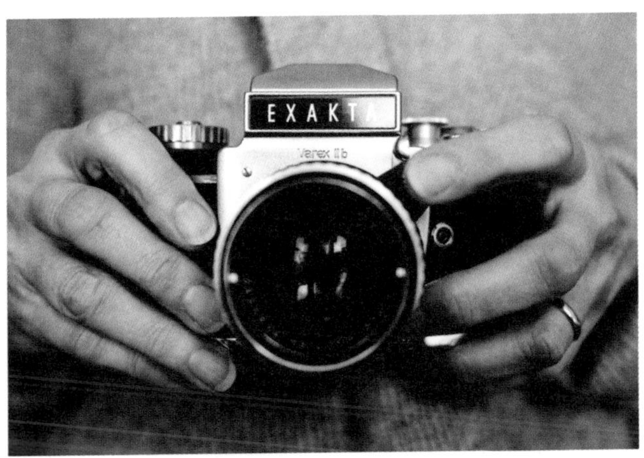
Varex IIb

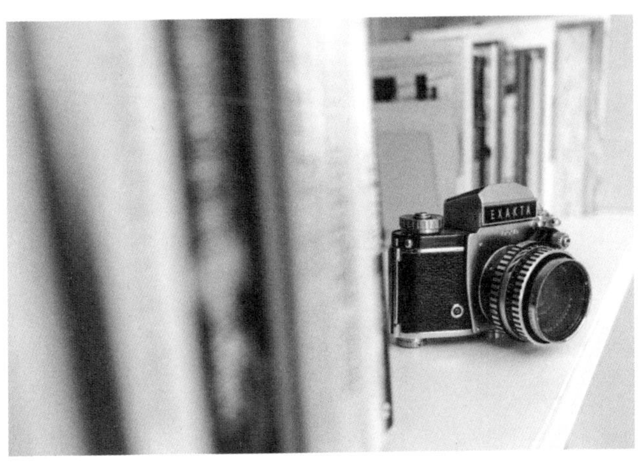
EXAKTA

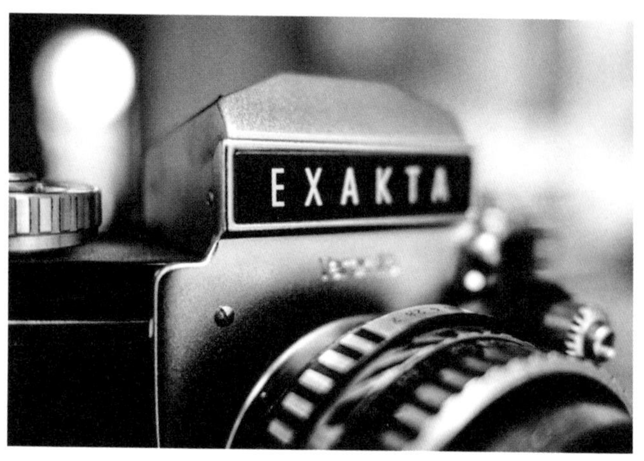
EXAKTA

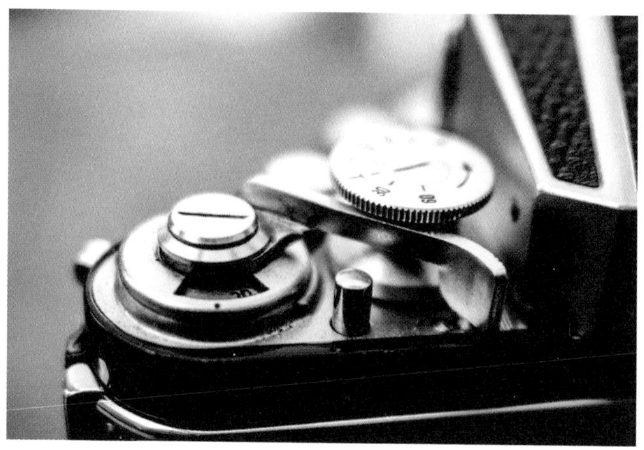

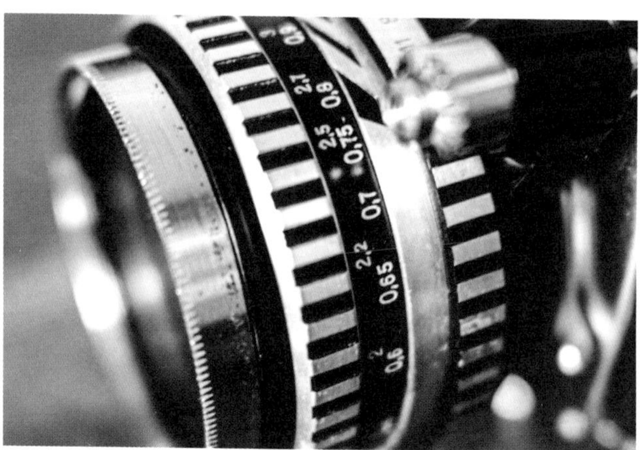
2,7
0,8
2,5
0,75
0,7
2,2
0,65
2
0,6

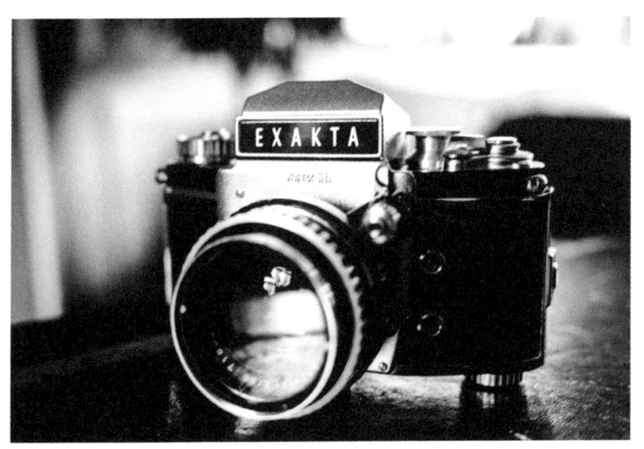
EXAKTA

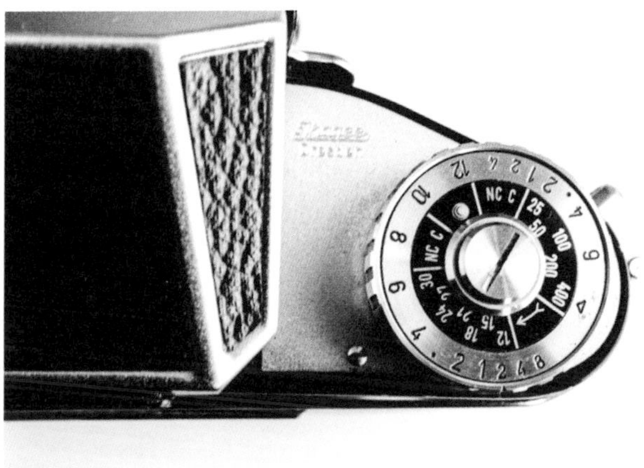
NC C
25
50
100
200
400
NC C
30
2 1 2 4 8

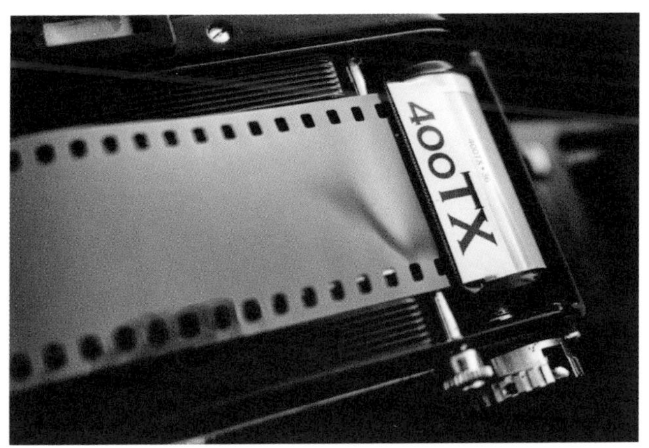
400TX

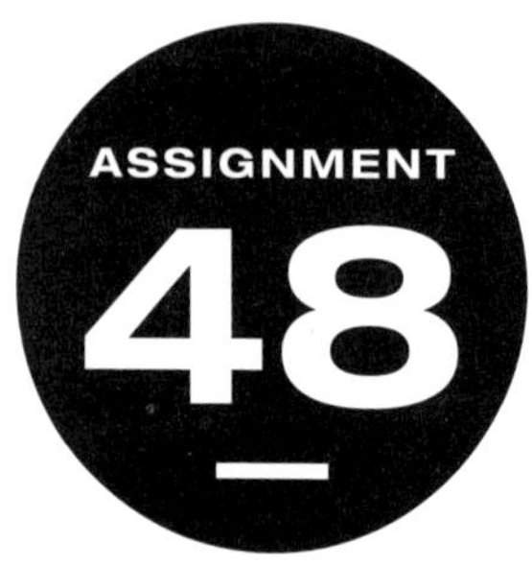

TECHNIQUE

- Always be looking out for good vantage points above you and be curious about what the higher vantage point could offer.
- If you're shooting at fairly close range, a wideangle lens (24 or 28mm) will emphasize the effect of height.
- Experiment a lot: play around with variations in height and with lines, perspective, angles, and shapes.

HIGH TIME

While it's natural to shoot everything with the viewfinder at eye level, it does feel a little complacent sometimes. If we let our eyes explore different perspectives, a whole new world of possibility opens up. One of those perspectives is shooting from above.

For this assignment, you'll need to find an elevated shooting position, such as a bridge, balcony, or rooftop, and shoot the world beneath you. The subject could be anything, but try to make sure your frame contains either human interest or a strong graphical element.

PRO TIPS

- If shadows are going to be part of your shot, you'll get much more interesting shapes early or late in the day when the sun is low.
- If you want to make your subject look small or insignificant, raising your shooting position by just one meter above your head will have a dramatic impact, particularly when using a wideangle lens.
- Consider adding a human element to give a sense of scale.

ASSIGNMENT JOURNAL

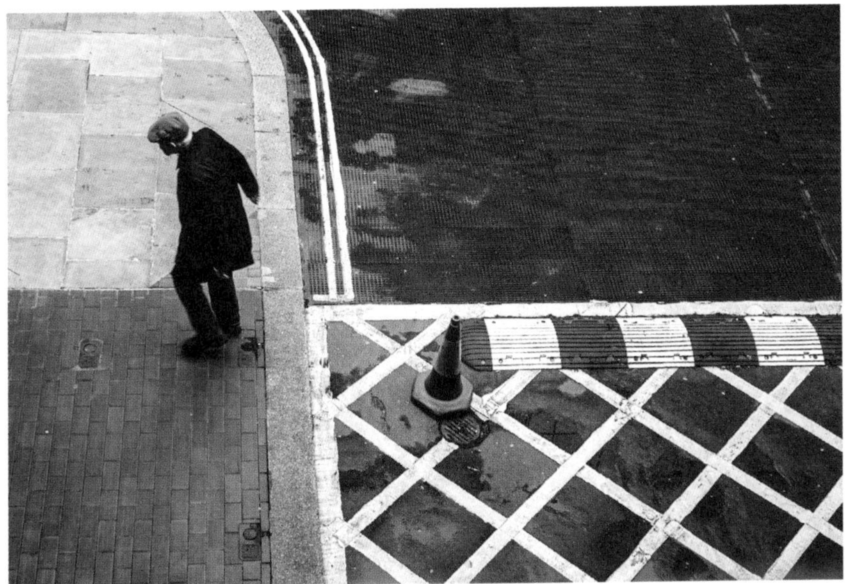

▲ *The softness of the human form contrasts with the harsh lines of the city landscape.*

▼ *Look for patterns and textures that wouldn't be apparent at eye level, like this confusion of railway tracks and overhead cables in Prague in the Czech Republic.*

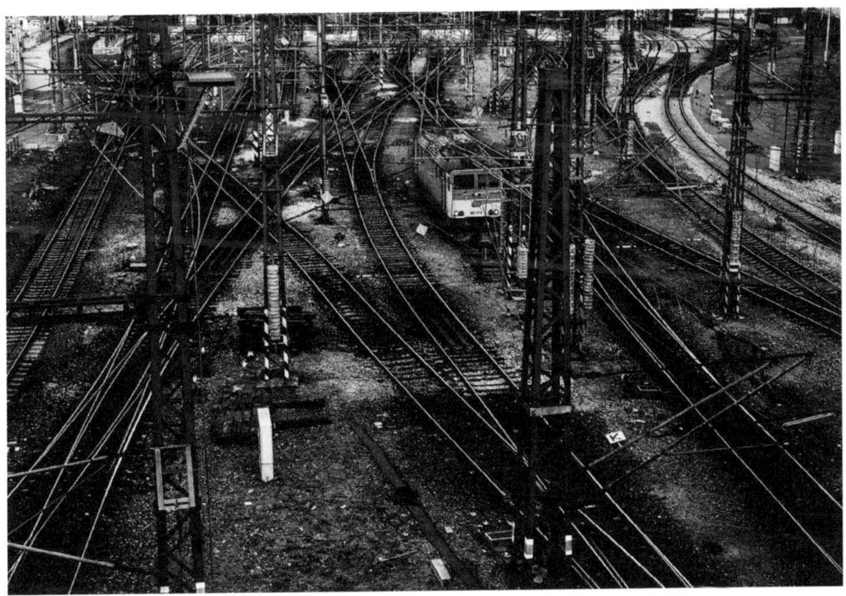

TECHNIQUE

- Your design needs to be attention-grabbing. Without the luxury of using color, your black-and-white design needs to be bold and striking. Don't be afraid to use negative space for impact.
- When shooting the image, consider where any graphics will be positioned in the final design, particularly the album title and artist's name.
- Your image can be shot in portrait or landscape orientation, but remember your final design should be square.
- Use your image-editing program to add text. Consider how the typeface "connects" with the artist and their music.

COVER ART

Whatever your taste in music, you'll probably be familiar with the album covers of your favorite band or artist. Designed to attract purchasers, album cover artwork is striking and designed with care.

This assignment gives you the chance to put yourself in the shoes of a commercial photographer, with a task that is as much about developing the concept as it is about shooting the image. Accomplished photographers have great conceptual skills, and here you'll need to think hard about how your concept will connect with the audience and create more album sales.

Your mission is to choose an artist and design a cover for their new album. The artist (or band) could be real or fictitious, and you can either redesign the cover for an existing album or invent your own.

Treat this as a commercial assignment and shoot a variety of options for your client to consider—a shortlist of eight would be ideal.

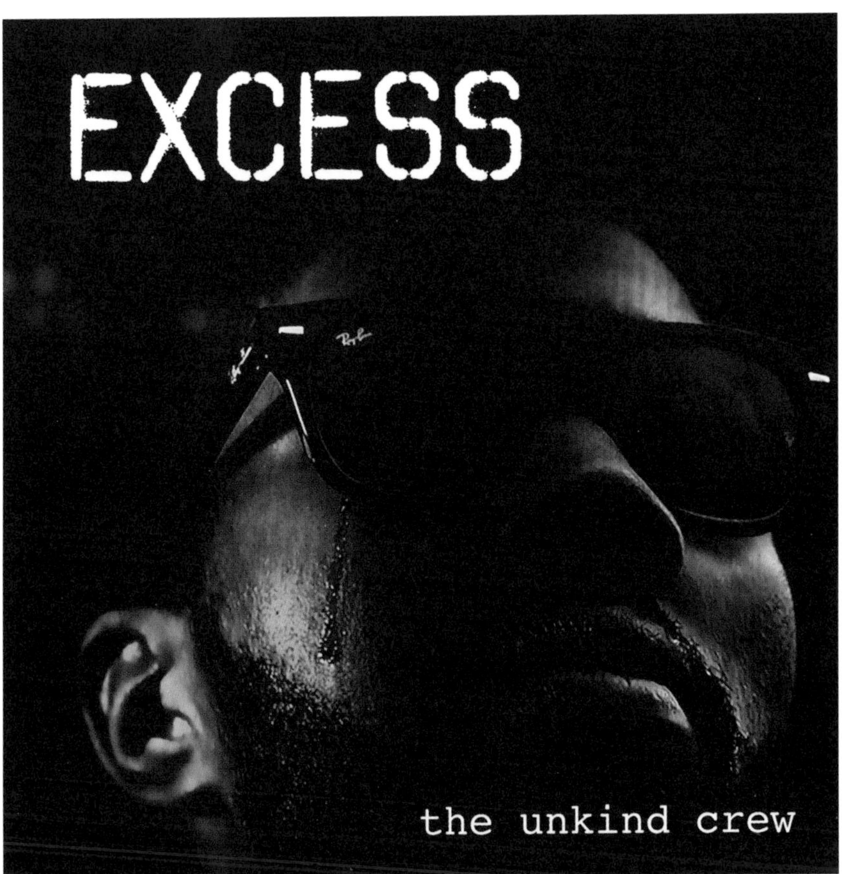

▲ *Strong, bold designs with striking graphics help sell albums.*

PRO TIPS

- Be careful to synchronize the tone of your image with the style of the music. For example, you wouldn't want a picture of a butterfly on the latest death-metal release.
- Consider the artist's target audience and how your image will resonate with them.
- Don't forget to look at some of your favorite album covers for inspiration.

ASSIGNMENT JOURNAL

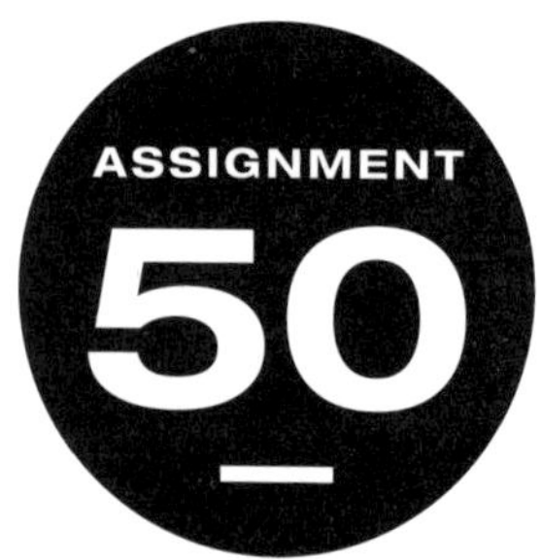

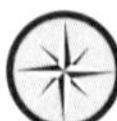

TECHNIQUE

- If the background doesn't contribute anything relevant, use a wide aperture to throw it out of focus.
- The lighting is critical and can have a dramatic effect on your image. Find the best viewpoint relative to the light to accentuate the key features and bring out the tree's character.
- Experiment with different focal lengths, from wideangle to medium telephoto.
- Consider how the tree's placement in the frame will affect the dynamics and mood of the shot. For example, a centered composition could suggest stature and importance; applying the Rule of Thirds could suggest tranquility or serenity; and a tree near the edge of the frame could induce feelings of unease or instability.

BRANCH OUT

This is a very straightforward assignment. Your brief is to take a portrait of a solitary tree. Photographed in isolation and without distractions, every tree has a unique character and "personality." It's your job to capture that personality in your photograph.

First, find your tree. Remember that it's a solitary tree you're looking for, not one in a group—and the lonelier, the better. Approach this as you would any other portrait: find the most interesting or flattering aspect, the best viewpoint, and the best light.

You could develop this assignment into a more enduring project by shooting the same tree at the same time of day and from the same position, every month of the year, which could make a great set of prints or postcards.

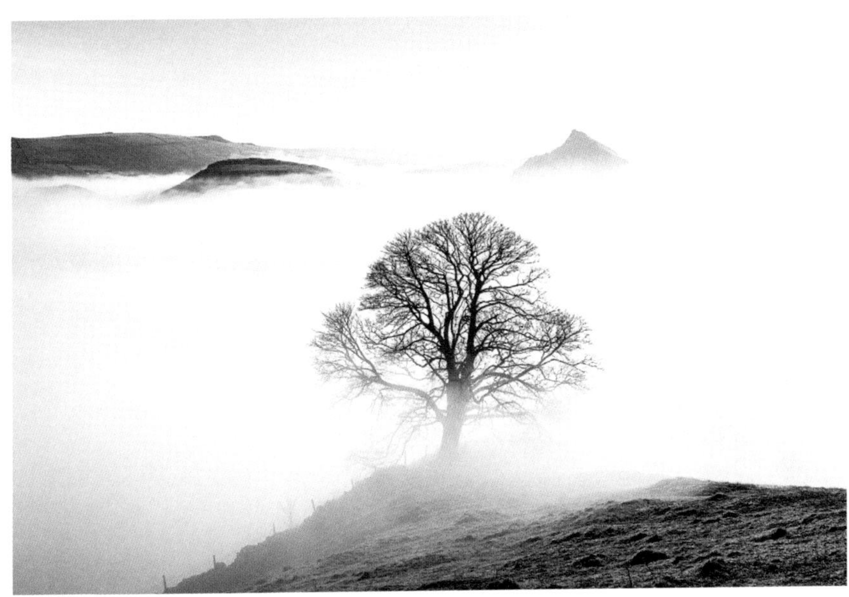

▲ *You could say this tree, standing alone on the windy hilltop, has a confident and independent "personality."*

PRO TIPS

- Once you have found your tree, do some research: when will it look at its best? When is it in bloom? What weather conditions will suit it best?
- Portraits are always easier if you know something about the personality of your subject, so get to know your tree!
- Look for textures and patterns to help bring out the tree's character.
- Some trees have a network of big roots that are visible above the ground. These can look great when shot from a low viewpoint with a wideangle lens.

ASSIGNMENT JOURNAL

PRO TIPS

- Don't rush it: a project like this takes time and it's often a mistake to complete it too quickly.
- Look for the unusual in the usual, the right thing in the wrong place, or something that just makes you smile.

TECHNIQUE

- Plan your concept in advance and stick to it, and have a target number of images to aim for. This will keep you focused and motivated.
- As you're working in black and white, you can't rely on color for separation, so you'll need well-defined shapes and tones.
- It's usually good to separate the object from the background, so open up the lens to its maximum aperture for a shallow depth of field.
- Be prepared to get your camera down to ground level to make the most of a crisp composition and/or the most favorable light.

LOST AND FOUND

Picasso did it. Dali did it. Henry Moore did it. In modern art, we use the term "found object" (translated from the French phrase "objet trouvé") to describe an object found by an artist, which, with little or no modification, is then presented as a work of art. As small children, we spend a lot of time looking down, examining the world around our feet, and that's exactly what you'll need to do to complete this assignment.

Your task is to create a collection of images of found objects with a central theme, and there are a number of ways you could approach this. You could choose a geographical area (maybe even one street) and spend a few weeks or months recording all the objects found in that area. Alternatively, you might like to focus on a particular type of object, such as bottles, fruit, or items of clothing. Consider basing your collection on a more abstract concept, looking for items with a common shape or form, or perhaps you could use the idea to make a point about a topic that interests you, such as plastic pollution on our beaches.

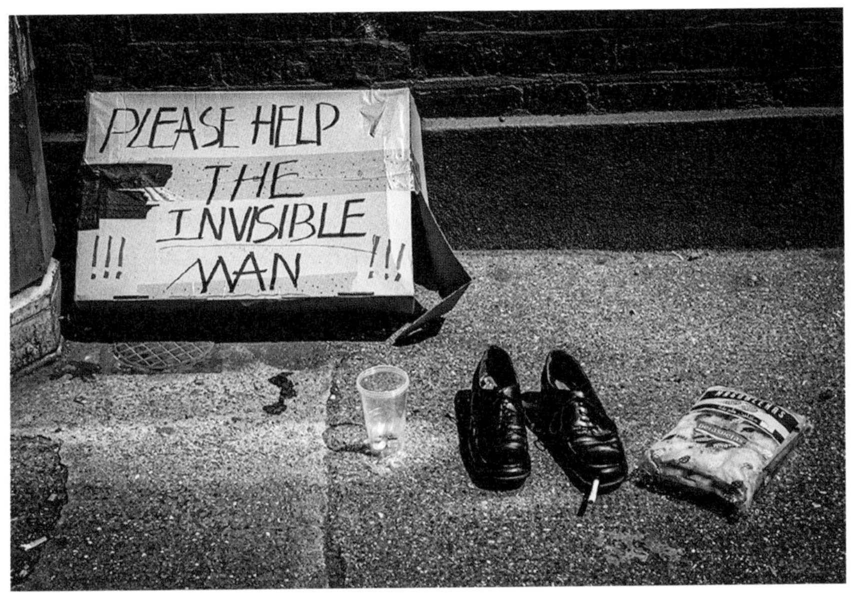

▲ *Sometimes everything is set up for you, like this lovely little tableau outside a store.*

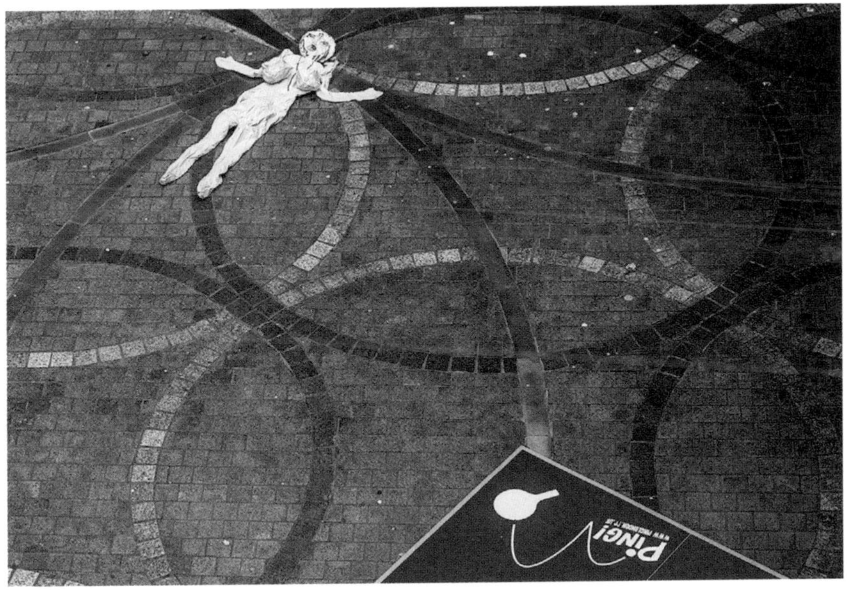

▲ *Shot outside a busy city library, here's an object that surely has a tale to tell. It adds to the intrigue when the object is discovered in an unlikely place.*

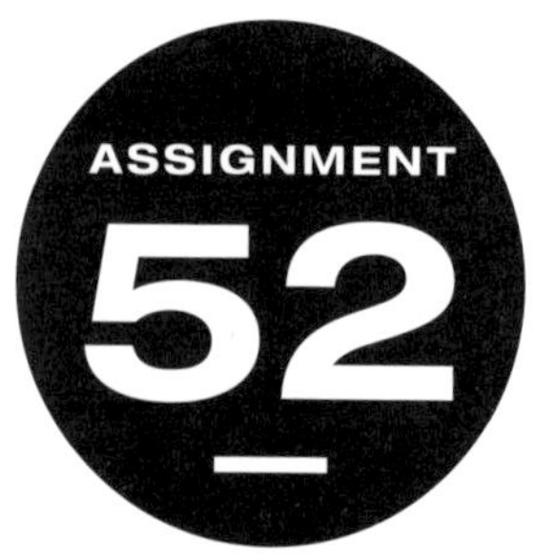

TECHNIQUE

- If you're including people in your images, try to have one solitary person and ensure that their demeanor or dress matches the mood of the image.
- Don't worry too much about technical perfection. This assignment is more about mood and feeling, than it is about the fine detail.
- Aim to convey a feeling of hopelessness or desolation—the bleaker, the better!

▶ *Using a red filter darkened the sky, creating a more moody shot of this derelict pub.*

GHOST TOWN

The Specials wrote about a derelict town in their seminal 1981 song, and what was topical then is still topical today. Businesses in towns and cities around the world are suffering from closure and decay.

Some projects lend themselves particularly well to the medium of black and white, and this is the perfect example, as stripping color out of the story presents an even bleaker landscape.

In this documentary assignment, your aim is to chronicle the decline of the town center—think closed stores, the absence of people, tumbleweed, and decaying buildings. Try to visualize this as a photoessay of six to eight images. Imagine it as a human interest story, appearing as a feature on the pages of a newspaper or magazine.

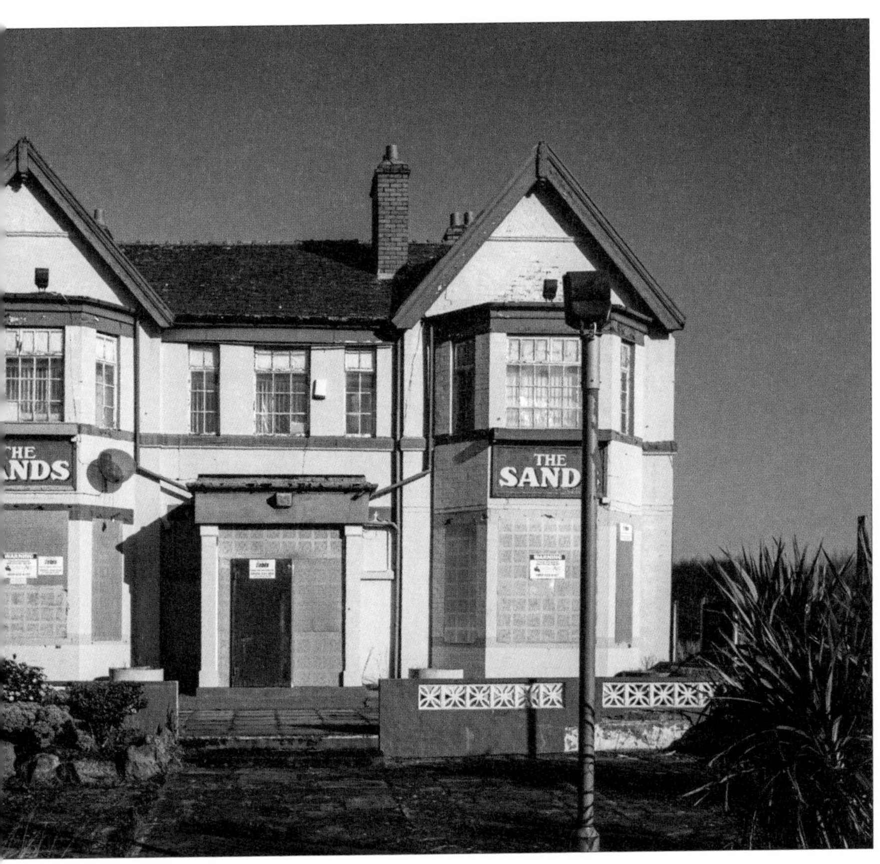

PRO TIPS

- Have a "hero" image, a shot that acts as the "anchor" and draws the viewer in. This should be the most striking picture of the series.
- Aim for variety: avoid too many shots of the same subject, such as boarded-up stores and buildings.

ASSIGNMENT JOURNAL

INDEX

First published 2021 by
Ammonite Press
an imprint of Guild of Master Craftsman Publications Ltd
Castle Place, 166 High Street, Lewes, East Sussex, BN7 1XU,
United Kingdom

Reprinted 2022

ISBN 978 1 78145 444 2

A catalog record for this book is available from the British Library.

Publisher: Jonathan Bailey
Design Manager: Robin Shields
Designer: Rhiann Bull
Editor: Laura Paton

Color reproduction by GMC Reprographics
Printed and bound in China

ACKNOWLEDGMENTS

To Johannah, Alex, and Maisie, whose ideas, support, and homemade treacle tarts have helped keep me going. Also, big "thank yous" to my editor, Laura Paton; to my friend and fellow Fujifilm ambassador, Chris Upton, for providing me with a couple of his terrific landscape images for this book; and to the team at Fujifilm UK. Bravo, you all played your part!

How was the book?
Please post your
feedback and photos:
#52AssignmentsBlack&White

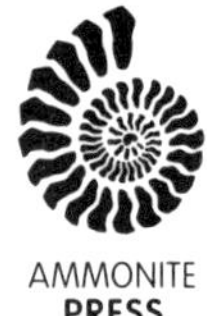

ammonitepress.com

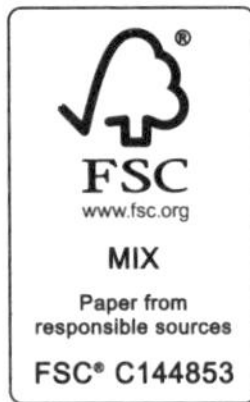